SUCCEED AT
PSYCHOMETRIC TESTING

PRACTICE TESTS FOR
CRITICAL VERBAL
REASONING

PETER S. RHODES

SUCCEED AT
PSYCHOMETRIC TESTING

**PRACTICE TESTS FOR
CRITICAL VERBAL
REASONING**

Hodder Arnold

A MEMBER OF THE HODDER HEADLINE GROUP

For order enquiries please contact Bookpoint Ltd, 130 Milton Park, Abingdon, Oxon OX14 4SB. Telephone: (44) 01235 827720. Fax: (44) 01235 400454. Lines are open from 9.00–18.00, Monday to Saturday, with a 24-hour message answering service. Details about our titles and how to order are available at www.hoddereducation.com

British Library Cataloguing in Publication Data
A catalogue record for this title is available from the British Library

ISBN-10: 0340 926724
ISBN-13: 978 0340 926 727

First published   2006
Impression number 10 9 8 7 6 5 4 3 2 1
Year   2010   2009   2008   2007   2006

The publisher has used its best endeavours to ensure that the URLs for external websites referred to in this book are correct and active at the time of going to press. However, the publisher and the author have no responsibility for the websites and can make no guarantee that a site will remain live or that the content will remain relevant, decent, or appropriate.

Typeset by Servis Filmsetting Ltd, Longsight, Manchester.
Printed in Great Britain for Hodder Education,
a division of Hodder Headline, 338 Euston Road, London NW1 3BH
by Cox & Wyman Ltd, Reading, Berkshire.

Hodder Headline's policy is to use papers that are natural, renewable and recyclable products and made from wood grown in sustainable forests. The logging and manufacturing processes are expected to conform to the environmental regulations of the country of origin.

Contents

Acknowledgements   vi

Foreword   vii

Chapter 1:   Introduction   1

Chapter 2:   Timed tests   24

Chapter 3:   Answers to timed tests   112

Chapter 4:   Explanations of timed tests   119

Chapter 5:   Diagnosis and further reading   148

Acknowledgements

I would like to thank Valerie Newton at OTL for her assistance in the compilation of this text.

Foreword

If anyone tells you that it is impossible to improve your score in a psychometric test, don't pay any attention. It isn't true.

A multi-million pound industry has developed based on the notion that psychometric tests yield accurate and true data about an individual's ability. While this is generally the case, test results can differ widely and are determined by a range of factors, including the test environment, the professionalism and experience of the test administrator, the level of confidence of the candidate on the day of the test, the candidate's familiarity with the testing process, and the amount of practice a candidate has had prior to the test.

As the industry develops, test-takers are becoming more informed about what is expected of them, and about what they should expect from the testing process. Increasingly, candidates are taking control of the process, and demonstrating that it is feasible to prepare for psychometric tests and to improve scores significantly.

This series of books was designed with you, the test-taker, in mind. In finding this book you have demonstrated a commitment to achieving your potential in the upcoming test.

Commitment and confidence play a large role in determining your level of success, and practice will help to build your confidence.

A common complaint from candidates is that they cannot find enough material to practise. This series aims to overcome this deficiency by providing you with chapter after chapter of timed tests for you to take under test conditions. The series covers many examples of question sets appropriate to the major test publishers, and will help you to prepare for numerical, verbal, logical, abstract and diagrammatic reasoning tests.

Chapter 1 offers you specific advice on how to prepare for your test. Once you have read through the instructions in Chapter 1, go straight to the timed tests in Chapter 2. Chapter 3 lists all the answers to the questions in Chapter 2 in one part, so that you can quickly check off the answers, and Chapter 4 provides you with the explanations. If you have time, wait a few days before retaking the tests – at least enough time to have forgotten the answers. In between taking and retaking the tests in this series, practise with other sources. You will find a list of these in Chapter 5.

Few people enjoy psychometric tests. Yet if psychometric tests are the major obstacle between you and your perfect job, it is worth spending some time learning how to get beyond this obstacle. You can be proactive in achieving your best score by practising as much as you can.

Finally, if you don't achieve your best score at your first attempt, try again. You may be pleasantly surprised by your results the second time around. Good luck!

Heidi Smith
Series Editor

The other titles in the series are:
Numerical Reasoning Intermediate
Numerical Reasoning Advanced
Verbal Reasoning Intermediate
Verbal Reasoning Advanced
Diagrammatic and Abstract Reasoning
Data Interpretation
The National Police Selection Process
The Armed Forces Entry Level

CHAPTER 1

Introduction

WHY READ THIS BOOK?

It arrives. The job advert could have been written with you in mind. You applied, and now you are through to the next stage. The letter informs you that as well as the interview there is also going to be a psychometric test – a test of your critical verbal reasoning. Your heart sinks. And you are starting to worry. You have not taken a test before or have not done one for years. Or worse still, the last time you took a test you were told you had not done very well.

But one of the best-kept secrets about psychological tests is that it is possible to improve your score quite dramatically.

Psychologists who devise tests and test publishers who publish them do not talk about this much. Publishers' test sales depend on their corporate clients having faith in the value of testing. They encourage organisations who purchase their materials to think that measuring aspects of someone's ability is as straight-forward as measuring their height or weight. But it is not. For example, if you were to measure your height today and tomorrow, next month, or two months' time you will get the same result. But if you were to take a psychometric test on different occasions, it is unlikely to produce the same results.

With psychological tests, scores change. This is because, unlike measuring height, a whole lot of factors go into producing your test score. For this reason, psychometric tests are based on the assumption that they give only a glimpse or an estimate of someone's 'true score'. Traditional psychometric theory suggests a person's score on any test is made up of his or her 'true score' – i.e. real level of ability – and 'junk'. Junk is made up of all the factors (such as anxiety, low expectations of success, lack of confidence, confusing instructions by the test administrator, etc.) which can all get in the way of you doing your best.

Unfortunately, the idea that a test score is essentially a 'sample' providing, at best, a probabilistic estimate of someone's ability is very often forgotten in organisational test usage. And often test scores are treated as if they are straightforwardly 'true', with little account taken of the degree of error they contain (e.g. that people taking the test had very different levels of experience with tests).

With this in mind, this book is partly about ensuring that, when you come to take the test, there is no 'junk' – nothing getting in the way of you doing yourself justice in the test. But the aim of this book goes beyond this relatively modest goal. Whilst traditional psychometric theory assumes there is a 'true score', some psychologists would argue there is no such thing.

In other words, there is no true score – no relatively fixed level of ability glimpsed (with some element of junk) in a psychometric test. What they would argue is that ability tests essentially measure discrete 'task skills' (i.e. the ability to do a specific task) rather than measuring more fundamental and fixed human capacities. And task skills are, by definition, much more malleable than the pervasive and fundamental human capacities which publishers claim are being measured.

This is particularly true when thinking about your critical verbal reasoning. When you were born your critical verbal reasoning was not, like some aspects of intelligence, 'hard wired' – a fundamental aspect of who you are and what you are potentially capable of achieving. Critical verbal reasoning is much more susceptible to development.

The aim of this book is therefore to enable you to improve your score on a critical verbal reasoning tests by:

a removing some of the well-documented factors likely to reduce your performance

b coaching you on the task skills involved in critical verbal reasoning tests.

SO HOW CAN I IMPROVE MY SCORE?

There is a great deal of research evidence that, unlike measuring height, scores on psychometric tests of ability are affected by a number of factors. There are at least five factors which this book can help with.

Expectation of success

There is a vast body of research demonstrating that one of the crucial determinants of your test performance is the extent to which you feel you are likely to do well.

This book is not intended as an academic text and so a detailed review of this evidence is not appropriate. To illustrate the importance of expectation of success, one study will suffice. In this carefully conducted study (reported in one of the more reputable academic journals), individuals were divided into two groups. Each group was required to do the same ability test. The only difference was that one group was given instructions which suggested they may find the test difficult. The other group was told they would find the test interesting and challenging. The hormone levels of individuals in each group were carefully monitored.

Even though the instructions differed by only a few words, the two groups appeared to go down completely different biochemical pathways. The 'interesting challenge' group filled up with hormones making it easier for them to focus their attention on the test. The 'difficult challenge' group went down a biochemical pathway which meant their blood streams filled up with hormones making them anxious, and this made it more difficult for them to focus their attention effectively.

This study vividly illustrates the importance of your expectations. How you feel about the test appears to have a profound physiological effect. If you feel confident and prepared you are more likely to go down a biochemical pathway that helps you focus than if you feel the test is likely to be difficult and challenging.

So, use this book to ensure you *feel* ready and prepared for the demands of the task. Do the practice tests and then, if necessary, do them again and again until you feel you are prepared.

Test sophistication

Another well-established factor likely to affect your perform-ance is your level of familiarity with tests. This was a big issue when the 11+ exam was compulsory in the UK. The outcome could affect the rest of a child's life. And so, not surprisingly, a cottage industry of teachers coaching the children of anxious parents sprang up. There was evidence at the time that this coaching had a significant effect on exam performance. I have anecdotal evidence of the impact of coaching. A colleague coached his daughter on the 11+ style exams, as the grammar schools in the county they lived in had retained the selective system. His daughter's initial performance placed her well outside of the top 25 per cent required to receive a place. After several attempts on different tests and coaching on the ratio-nales of typical questions, his daughter's performance steadily improved. She won her place at the grammar school.

For some time, test publishers have encouraged their clients to send out 'practice sets'. This was largely as a result of pressure from the Commission for Racial Equality who felt that for some minority groups the experience of being tested was extremely alien and that the example questions publishers normally included in their test booklets were not comprehensive enough to create a level playing field.

It may well be that you have already received yours or will receive a set in due course. These sets usually provide only a very small number of practice questions. The evidence suggests the more coaching the better. So, in addition to the materials you receive from the publisher, the practice items available to you in this book will help you improve your performance even more.

These practice tests are particularly useful when used in conjunction with this book. The practice test will indicate what the 'item style' is – the type of questions you will be sitting on the day. This text covers all of the major item styles. So it is possible to restrict your practice to the part of this book which resembles the questions you have been sent.

If you have not been sent a practice set, do not be afraid to telephone the organisation and ask for one. Providing practice sets is regarded as 'best practice' by personnel practitioners. They also normally do not cost anything as they come free with the pack of answer sheets.

Speed

Related to both these issues is the fundamental one of your 'response strategy' during the test. Some people prefer accuracy to speed; others will trade off some accuracy for getting through more questions. Generally, accuracy is not really taken into account when interpreting your test performance in organisational settings. This would take test interpretation into a much more 'qualitative' area similar to that employed in educational and clinical settings, where thinking style and how someone coped with the materials (e.g. how frustrated someone seemed) are as important as what score was achieved.

In organisational usage, interpreting test performance is more straightforward. The issue is simply how many you got right in a fixed amount of time compared to a comparison group. Only one type of critical reasoning test permits an untimed administration which allows everyone to complete the test.

So more often than not this means three golden rules apply:

- always trade off accuracy for speed (although not to the point where you are not paying sufficient attention to questions)

- always do as many questions as possible

- never spend too much time on any one question.

The higher your expectation of success and your familiarity with test items, the more items you are likely to be able to attempt.

The importance of speed becomes clearer if we consider the way your performance on the day will be interpreted. One of the sad realities of life is that most of us are average. And this means virtually all tests have the same distribution of test scores (see Figure 1.1). Most scores bunch up around some average point. It is of course the same with height, weight or shoe size. The fact that we all tend to have roughly the same size feet, with only a relatively small number of individuals having extremely big or small feet makes stocking shoes easier: more shoes of an average size will be required.

This characteristic normal 'distribution' of scores has very profound implications which you are able to take advantage of. What the 'hump' in the middle of Figure 1.1 shows is that most scores tend to bunch up around a middle point.

The statistic which most organisations in the UK use to interpret test performance is the 'percentile'. The percentile is not to be confused with a percentage. The percentile refers to the proportion of a comparison group who would get the same score

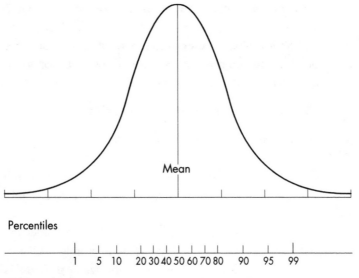

Figure 1.1 The normal distribution and percentiles

(or a worse score) than you. This sounds like an odd definition. But it means you are on the 45 percentile if 45 per cent
of people in the comparison group have either got the same
score or did worse than you and that 55 per cent of the comparison group have done better.

There are numerous problems with percentiles. For example,
they give psychometric tests a spurious air of accuracy they do
not deserve. Another problem is that percentiles massively overstate small differences in scores in the middle of the range (see
how they are bunched in Figure 1.1). Unfortunately, most of the
problems with percentiles, especially the tendency to overstate
differences in the middle of the range, are often ill-understood
by personnel practitioners.

To illustrate this, take a look at the data in Table 1.1. This is used to interpret candidates' performance on a critical verbal reasoning test collected by an assessment consultancy, OTL, which is similar to that provided by test publishers to organisations and used to assess the performance of candidates.

Table 1.1

Candidate's score	Percentile
39	75
38	70
37	65
36	50
35	45
34	40
33	35
32	30
31	25

In this typical data, only eight points separate those on the 75th percentile from those on the 25th. The test has 56 questions. But percentiles understate differences at the extremes so there is only a two percentile difference between those who get 44 and those who get 56 (97th and 99th percentiles). So all the 'action' in percentile terms is in the middle range. If you think about this, if you are in the centre of the range (which is where most of us are), it only needs a slight improvement to shift your score, *in percentile terms*, dramatically. For example, only four more questions attempted and answered correctly could take you from the 40th to the 70th percentiles on this particular critical verbal reasoning test. Some norms produce even more dramatic increments than this. The more the score is interpreted against a 'restricted group', such as managers or supervisors, the more pronounced this effect is likely to be.

The reality is that these relatively insignificant differences in scores tend to be over-interpreted in organisational settings. A selection panel would assume that the candidate on the 70th percentile is significantly better than the one who is 'only' on the 40th percentile. But the difference could be the result of one candidate making two lucky guesses and somebody else having two unlucky guesses.

The key point here is *that for most of us a small shift in response rate can have a significant impact on the percentile we achieve.*

So the more practice you have, the more confidence you will develop, and the more rapidly you will be able to progress through any set of questions.

Speed is important in most tests but it is, as suggested, particularly important in high level tests – i.e. those designed for use with supervisory and managerial groups. In these groups scores are invariably more 'bunched up', as there tends to be less of a difference between individuals than there normally is within the general population. As all critical verbal reasoning tests are 'high level' tests designed to be used at supervisory level and above, this point is particularly salient.

Interpretation of the task

Another key determinant of your score is your understanding of what is required of you by the test. At a basic level, this means ensuring you understand where the answer block is. Yes – people do sometimes fill in the wrong block! One of the most popular critical verbal reasoning tests has an answer sheet with five answer blocks, the first of which is offset to the right-hand side of the double sheet. This means candidates used to starting on the left of a document will tend to look at the first block on the left-hand side.

It also means ensuring you are clear how you are supposed to fill in the answer sheet to indicate correct responses, e.g. whether you are supposed to be circling, underlining, crossing out or ticking.

At a more complex level, *interpretation of the task* is about the extent to which you have been 'psychologically engaged' by the complexity of the exercise and understand exactly how the test works – what the 'rules' are. This is particularly crucial with critical verbal reasoning. Critical verbal reasoning tests will often start with a complex example. This is a paragraph of information and a number of questions which involve you considering whether, on the basis of the information given, a statement is true, false or you cannot tell.

But of course, true, false and cannot tell have very specific meanings. For example, does 'cannot tell' mean within the context of this passage or based more generally on what you know about the subject matter? Starting the test without really understanding what the 'rules of the game' are will mean you are likely to produce a test score well below what your notional 'true score' is.

This book helps here because all of the major item styles for critical verbal reasoning tests are described and explained.

If, however, the employer is using a test from an obscure source which this book does not simulate, then it is important to ensure the test administrator does his or her job effectively. If you do not understand why you have got an example wrong, or indeed if you have got an example correct but are not 100 per cent certain why it is the correct answer, then say so. There is no shame or embarrassment attached to getting examples wrong or seeking clarification. In fact, a good administrator ought to create an environment where you are encouraged to ask questions.

The environment

Environmental factors have a huge impact on your performance. It is important that you are tested in a room with adequate heating, ventilation, lighting and free from interruptions. Whilst this might seem obvious, I have encountered organisations who test in public areas, such as reception and corridors, or use the office of a manager who is away for the day – but where the phone keeps ringing.

Unlike your familiarity with tests and your expectation of success, you have less immediate control over these factors. The quality of the environment is the test administrator's responsibility. If he or she has been properly trained and is aware of the responsibility to create an environment which is, for example, free from distraction, then they ought to act in order to minimise any distractions which occur.

Do not be afraid to complain and point out any deficiencies in testing conditions. Most test publishers produce a 'test log' and include it with the answer sheets. This encourages test administrators to note anything which might affect your test performance. What is in the test log should be taken into account when interpreting your performance.

WHAT IS CRITICAL VERBAL REASONING?

Many people think psychometric tests are 'flavour of the month' or the 'latest bandwagon' management have jumped on. This might surprise you, but the first critical verbal reasoning test was published in 1937, is still in print in a new edition and is still technically the best measure of critical thinking.

One of the criticisms of psychometric tests is they are often trying to measure poorly defined concepts. Recent examples of this would include 'emotional intelligence' and 'learning styles'. But in the same way that it is difficult to differentiate 'emotional intelligence' from other aspects of our personality such as sensitivity and empathy, it is similarly not immediately apparent what the difference is between critical verbal reasoning and related concepts such as verbal reasoning. The concept of critical verbal reasoning is a prime example in psychometrics where the meaning is not immediately obvious.

Verbal reasoning tests are measures of verbal intelligence – the ability to perceive verbally expressed relationships. They are essentially 'blotting paper' tests, assessing your ability to absorb verbally expressed information, to go beyond the simple meaning of words and grasp concepts. A typical verbal

reasoning question might involve filling in the blanks from a set of options to a question like:

_____ is to night as breakfast is to _____

A verbal reasoning test would therefore give an estimate of an individual's educability. In the US the SAT tests, used for University selection alongside a student's academic achievement, comprise a significant verbal reasoning component.

So how is critical verbal reasoning different to ordinary verbal intelligence? The word critical is perhaps a difficulty here, as we tend to use the word in a number of ways in our language, often to indicate a negative attitude. With critical verbal reasoning the word indicates not so much a negative approach but an evaluative one. A definition of critical verbal reasoning might be *the ability to evaluate, dispassionately and objectively, persuasive and emotive information.*

Critical verbal reasoning tests are therefore attempts to sample what is increasingly seen as a 'crunch skill' in management. Managers are often dependent on what others are telling them. They have to make decisions and judgements about other people's opinions. For example, a team manager in a Social Care and Health Directorate of a local authority will be presented with evidence and a recommendation for a particular decision about a child (taking him or her into care, leaving the child with the parent(s)). There will inevitably be a good deal of emotive content and assumptions being made (for example about the likelihood of any improvement in the care of the child by his or her family).

So critical verbal reasoning tests are an attempt to simulate situations like this, where a manager has been presented with a report which has been prepared by someone who may know more about a subject than he or she does. In addition, the report may be arguing very persuasively and perhaps even emotively (trying to trigger feelings about issues) attempting to get option B chosen over options A and C.

To be effective, the manager needs to be able to put beliefs and prejudices to one side and look at the evidence dispassionately. The manager needs to ask these questions: Do the conclusions really follow from the analysis? Is the analysis itself valid (as opposed to being built on vague, unsupported assertions)? Is the argument littered with hidden assumptions?

In short, what a critical verbal reasoning test is attempting to assess is whether you or any manager taking the test can tell the difference between a good and a bad argument.

The test score therefore provides some evidence about your ability to evaluate information coming from your team. It also provides some clues about your ability to brief your own manager and whether, in a senior management team or project group, you would be able to inspect the proposals of colleagues and so contribute when considering issues outside of your own immediate corporate portfolio.

Critical verbal reasoning appears to be the result of a complex amalgam of traits. Some of us simply seem to have more 'critical' personalities and are instinctively less susceptible to poor or emotive argument. But part of our ability to reason critically comes from skill and experience. It is something we do all the time.

What is clear is that critical reasoning is not a 'fixed capacity', not an unvarying personal quality reflecting our innate intelligence fixed at the moment of conception. It is possible to do something about our critical verbal reasoning.

WHY AM I BEING ASKED TO DO A CRITICAL VERBAL REASONING TEST?

The description of critical verbal reasoning above suggested it is relevant in selection for most supervisory and managerial roles. In fact critical verbal reasoning tests have become the 'default' test of choice and are used almost unthinkingly irrespective of the job's demands. A famous example of this in the UK was when British Railways chose to use critical verbal reasoning tests to select train drivers. Seven Asian railway guards applying to be train drivers complained they had been discriminated against as English was not their first language and that the test was irrelevant to performance as a train driver. They won their claim and won damages.

More generally the critical verbal reasoning test is relevant if the role you are applying for involves:

- Complex decision-making

- Strategy/policy formulation

- Business planning

- Contributing to project groups

- Being a member of a management team and having to contribute outside your own immediate corporate portfolio.

If the job you are applying for involves none of these things, the test is of little value in indicating how you will cope. The test administrator on the day will therefore struggle to make the links between the test and the job role clear. And this is when test usage brings itself into disrepute – testing for the sake of it.

The purpose of this book is to provide you with examples of tests which closely simulate the demands of the tests you will be given.

But before we look at specific examples of critical reasoning tests, it is useful to make some general points which will help you irrespective of the particular test you are required to take on the day.

It is worth remembering that in undertaking a critical reasoning test you are being asked to demonstrate an ability you are probably already using. When we are judging the coherence of an argument in a newspaper or assessing whether a recommendation in a report can be acted on, we are using the same skills that are sampled by any of the critical reasoning tests you will be facing.

Whether we realise this or not when we are judging arguments, we are essentially having to recognise and evaluate:

● Reasons

● Assumptions

● Conclusions

So in everyday life we are already having to work at distinguishing reasons, conclusions and assumptions in what people are telling us.

With critical reasoning tests what part of an argument counts as a reason, conclusion or assumption is normally identified for us. But whilst this helps – as we do not have to spend time working out what the reasons and conclusions are supposed to be – what can be confusing is that most critical verbal reasoning tests require us to do two things which we do not normally do when evaluating arguments in real life:

- Assume that statements in passages are true
- Suspend our everyday knowledge and beliefs.

This can be the most difficult thing a critical verbal reasoning test requires us to do. In the earlier example, the team manager in the Social Care and Health Directorate would have had a great deal of context available to him or her when assessing the team manager's recommendation. He or she might have had some views about the credibility of the source based on how effective the social worker preparing the report has been in the past. This would provide an important general context for evaluating the recommendation.

The reason for the absence of this in a critical reasoning test is that part of what is being measured is our ability to suspend our beliefs and prejudices and interpret the information in front of us dispassionately and objectively. So whatever you believe you generally know about an issue, put it to one side and focus on what is in front of you in the passage.

Critical reasoning tests, at least the ones you are most likely to be exposed to, have three approaches to sampling critical reasoning skills.

The Watson Glaser Critical Thinking Appraisal – the 'mother' of all critical reasoning tests and still technically the most comprehensive measure of it – utilises a specific model of critical reasoning. It samples five facets of critical thinking separately:

- Inference: drawing conclusions from observed or supposed facts.

- Recognition of assumptions: choosing between assumptions which are and which are not made in an argument.

- Deduction: distinguishing between conclusions which necessarily follow and those which do not from statements presumed to be true (i.e. are true by definition).

- Interpretation: distinguishing between conclusions which follow logically, beyond reasonable doubt, from a statement (i.e. are probably true).

- Evaluation of arguments: judging the strength or weakness of arguments.

Most of the other tests you are likely to be exposed to, those produced for example by the publishers ASE and SHL, use a common item format. These present individuals with a brief passage, followed by some related statements which have the effect of making each statement the conclusion of an argument. The task is then to assess whether a conclusion does or does not follow, or whether there is not enough information.

One variant of this is to provide a significant amount of information in a separate information card which has to be analysed.

One further type of item is included in this text. This involves presenting longer passages of information which require the candidate to make a number of the Watson Glaser range of judgements, but this time all on the same piece of information. This approach is found, for example, in the online critical reasoning test published by Tests Direct.

This book is designed to provide you with practice examples of the test you will have to take. Whatever test you eventually take, there are a number of general tips which are worth remembering.

General tips for taking any critical reasoning tests

The majority of critical reasoning tests involve the True/False/Can't tell format. In these, the questions you respond to are actually the conclusions to arguments. And it is useful to remember this. In fact each question you are asked to consider could be prefaced with a word which would indicate you are being presented with an argument and a conclusion.

So each of the questions could start with, 'so', 'hence', 'therefore' or 'thus'. In fact it may be useful to write these words down on a piece of paper to remind yourself that the questions require you to judge the soundness of the conclusions.

Conclusions to arguments can be true (or false) by definition. So there will be questions which involve restating reasons provided in the passage. If the conclusion (question statement) is restating a reason which is provided in the passage the answer must be true. ASE's first graduate test, for example, consists entirely of these questions. All that is required is identifying statements (reasons) which have already been stated in the passage.

If the conclusion contradicts a reason stated in the passage, the answer must be false.

However, critical reasoning tests require you not only to evaluate judgements which are true or false by definition, but also to consider what is (and is not) logically implied by the information in a passage.

To do this, you need to remember these rules:

1 Look back at the passage. Does it contain a reason, or reasons which are directly relevant to the conclusion? Reasons may or may not (and normally do not in psychometric tests) have marker words in front of them such as 'because', 'for', 'if', or 'since'. So it helps to imagine whether these words could be put in front of sentences. If you can put these words in front of the sentences in the passage then you have identified a reason, which might support the conclusion.

2 Reasons have to be relevant to a conclusion. Do they support the conclusion? Critical reasoning tests make this a little easier than when evaluating arguments in real life as we are normally asked to assume what is in the passage is true. So we do not have to worry about assessing the reliability and expertise of the source. Instead all we need to consider is: does the conclusion really follow from the reason(s) given for it? One quick mental check here is whether you would be prepared to act on the conclusion. If so, the answer must be true.

3 'Can't tell' responses are those where the conclusion is not true or false by definition and where reasons are not directly relevant. Thus, generally when in doubt, can't tell is normally the correct response. But remember to ignore what you may or may know about a subject. Critical reasoning tests often involve subjects that you may have strong feelings about. The Watson Glaser, for example has questions about democracy, trade unions, education, welfare and education. So whatever you may instinctively want to conclude, remember to suspend your beliefs and look at the reasons dispassionately and objectively.

4 Some tests such as the CRTV (ASE) and the Watson Glaser involve identifying assumptions. Think of an assumption as an unstated reason which may or may not support a conclusion. So an assumption is essentially a missing step in an argument. The way to approach these questions is again to put a conclusion word in front of the question which is the proposed assumption: hence, so, therefore or thus. Then ask yourself: does the assumption you are having to judge represent a directly-relevant reason for making this conclusion? Again, in your head it may be worth prefacing the assumptions with reason markers (because, since, for, as, and if).

5 Some tests such as the Watson Glaser involve making what appear at first sight to be more fine-grained distinctions: true, probably true, insufficient data, probably false and false. However, this framework is essentially the same as the distinctions we have already discussed. The true and false questions involve conclusions which either clearly restate or clearly contradict reasons provided in the passage. The probably true and probably false categories are those where the reasons stated in the passage are relevant and would either support or tend to refute the conclusion. The insufficient data category is the equivalent of can't tell.

The following chapter presents you with a range of critical reasoning tests. Each simulates an item style you are likely to encounter on the day.

CHAPTER 2

Timed tests

TEST 1

Section 1: Analysis

You will need to refer to the information on the next few pages in order to do the questions in Section 1. It may be useful therefore to photocopy these pages so that you can have the question and the information in front of you at the same time. But do not worry if you do not have access to a photocopier, it is still possible to do the questions. If you do photocopy the information do not study it at this point. Now go on and read the instructions for the analysis section and do the practice questions. Do not look at the information yet.

TERMS AND CONDITIONS OF EMPLOYMENT

Working Hours

Operative/warehouse   8.00am–4.00pm

Office   8.30am–4.30pm

Lunch Break

One hour, which must be taken between 11.30am and 2.00pm.

Annual Leave Allowance

The statutory annual leave is 20 working days. This rises to 25 days after three years' service and 30 days after ten years' service.

Health and Safety

Health and Safety Policy must be strictly observed at all times. Amendments to Health and Safety Policy as required by the Health and Safety Executive will be notified on the company intranet. All employees must undergo Health and Safety Training during the induction day which is provided on day one of your employment. Any failure to comply with Health and Safety requirements will result in Disciplinary Action.

Smoking Policy

As part of our Health and Safety Policy smoking is not allowed in any area of the company buildings. The only exception to this is in the staff bar.

Staff Discount

Company employees are entitled to a 40 per cent discount on the recommended retail price of products.

Pay

Managerial grade employees: monthly in arrears. Payment made last Friday of the month.

Other grades: weekly in arrears, payment made on Friday.

Travel/Subsistence Claims

Employees can recover standard class cost for rail journeys undertaken on company business. However those who have company cars must use these unless there is a clear reason for choosing to use the train.

Accommodation and expenses are reimbursed on production of receipts at the standard rates which are displayed on the company intranet.

Air travel needs to be authorised and arranged in advance by the Senior Finance Officer.

Car Parking/Visitors

Car parking facilities are available to employees in the designated areas at the back of the warehouse and at the front of the factory. The area outside of the office building is reserved for managers at director level. Car parking permits need to be displayed and are obtainable from the Human Resources department.

Those who are arranging to receive visitors need to ensure they obtain a permit. Their cars should be parked in spaces available outside the office building.

Social Amenities

Employees automatically become members of the Social Club. Facilities available to club members include:

Restaurant

The restaurant is subsidised and provides a range of freshly-prepared hot and cold meals during the lunch period (11.30am– 2.00pm). It also has snack food and drinks service available from 8.30am–11.00am and 3.00pm–4.00pm during the week.

Bar and Club Room Facilities

The club room is open each evening, from 6.30pm until 11.00pm, for employees. It is possible for employees to bring guests. However, to comply with licensing laws, guests need to be signed in on arrival.

Private Functions

By arrangement with the Club Steward, it is possible to book the restaurant or the club room for private functions on Saturday and Sunday lunchtimes. Where catering is required, please ensure the Steward is given at least one week's notice.

Sports Facilities

Employees are entitled to utilise our discounted membership rate at the David Lloyd Sports Centre. This can be done by

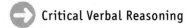

presenting the membership manager at the centre with your company pass.

Social Events

A number of social events are arranged throughout the year by the Club Committee. These can be viewed on the company intranet or on the notice board in the restaurant.

Club Committee

The Steward is responsible for the running of the restaurant and the club room on a day-to-day basis. However, it is possible for employees to become more involved by joining the Club Committee. Membership is a good way of getting more involved in the planning and the type of events arranged by the club. Two vacancies on the committee become available each year. Committee meetings take place once a month. The Committee is responsible for major decisions affecting club policies. Any employee wishing to raise a matter of concern should do so in writing and forward it to the Committee Chair. Current committee members' names are available on the company intranet and on the restaurant notice board.

Instructions and practice questions for Section 1: Analysis

In this section you will need to interpret the information in the Terms and Conditions of Employment. Each question is a statement. You need to answer:

● **True**, if the statement follows from or is implied by the information in the document

● **False**, if the statement contradicts what is given in the document

● **Can't tell**, if you cannot tell from the information in the document if the statement is true or false.

Before you start the first test, try these two practice questions. Study the information in the Terms and Conditions of Employment, and answer True, False or Can't tell.

P1 The company has arranged discounts for membership at other Sports Clubs.

True/False/Can't tell

P2 There are some employees working in the warehouse, who have not had Health and Safety Training.

True/False/Can't tell

You should have answered Can't tell for question P1 as there is no actual reference to other facilities. The answer to question P2 is False, as those working in the warehouse underwent the compulsory Health and Safety training on day one.

You will need a stopwatch, as this is a timed test. Now turn to pages 31–34 and answer the following questions. **You have nine minutes to do this section**.

Section 1: Questions

1 Some members of the Social Club are not company employees.

True/False/Can't tell

2 Employees need a parking permit.

True/False/Can't tell

3 New managerial employees starting work on Monday 15th will have to wait eleven days before getting paid.

True/False/Can't tell

4 Some non-compliance with Health and Safety is overlooked by managers.

True/False/Can't tell

5 Smoking in the warehouse will lead to disciplinary action.

True/False/Can't tell

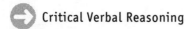

6 The Social Club Steward is a member of the Club Committee.

True/False/Can't tell

7 The restaurant as a business makes a loss.

True/False/Can't tell

8 Some employees have more than 30 days holiday.

True/False/Can't tell

9 Staff can buy company goods at 40 per cent of the recommended retail price.

True/False/Can't tell

10 The Social Club Committee has a stable membership.

True/False/Can't tell

11 Social Club Committee membership is actively encouraged by the company.

True/False/Can't tell

12 Some club members are not interested in joining the Committee.

True/False/Can't tell

13 The Club Steward has a major say in major decisions taken by the club.

True/False/Can't tell

14 Employees do not need to take up their sports memberships.

True/False/Can't tell

15 More staff at managerial level take up their sports memberships.

True/False/Can't tell

16 Some managers have to park their cars by the warehouse.

True/False/Can't tell

17 All cars outside the office are Directors' cars.

True/False/Can't tell

18 Factory staff have their lunch break before office staff.

True/False/Can't tell

19 Some employees have more than ten years' service.

True/False/Can't tell

20 There are no days each month when all staff are paid on the same day.

True/False/Can't tell

21 Employees can arrange their own accommodation when travelling on business.

True/False/Can't tell

Instructions and practice questions for Section 2: Evaluation

In this test each question consists of two parts. In the first you are told something which two new employees (Henry and Harriet) believe to be the case. In the second you are given some information (marked*) which comes to their attention. You have to decide what influence this information would have upon their belief.

You could answer:

● **Supports**, if the new information supports their belief

● **Goes against**, if the new information goes against their belief

● **No bearing**, if the new information has no bearing on their conclusion.

Now try these practice questions:

P1 Henry believes that office managers think team spirit is important.

*Henry finds out that office managers are going on a team-building course

Supports/Goes against/No bearing

P2 Harriet believes one of her team has a very poor attitude to work.

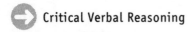 Critical Verbal Reasoning

*She notices that this team member sometimes arrives five minutes late for work.

Supports/Goes against/No bearing

The answer to P1 is Supports, since it is reasonable to assume that if managers are going on a team-building course then office managers do consider team spirit important.

The answer to P2 is No bearing, since being five minutes late for work is not really evidence for a team member having a very poor attitude to work.

Now Turn Over. **You have 6 minutes to do this section.**

Section 2: Questions

1 Henry believes the company is trying to improve its sales to Latin American countries.

*He is told one of his colleagues has been sent to a Venezuelan trade exhibition.

Supports/Goes against/No bearing

2 Harriet thinks Henry is interested in the company's current market position.

*Henry does not want to read an article she has spotted in the *Financial Times* about the company's performance.

Supports/Goes against/No bearing

3 Harriet believes that her manager is the longest serving member of staff.

*She finds out that her manager is due to retire in three years' time whereas the Operations Manager is retiring next year.

Supports/Goes Against/No bearing

4 Harriet believes the company was correct to focus its marketing on its more expensive premium range last year.

*She reads an article in the papers which indicates the company is making more profit.

Supports/Goes against/No bearing

5 Henry thinks the distribution centre may be closed down next year.

*He overhears a conversation between two managers complaining about the cost of local business rates for the building.

Supports/Goes against/No bearing

6 Harriet believes that the difference in the costs associated with producing the economy and premium branded goods are related to the quality of the metals used.

*She is told that the premium branded goods have a much higher quality metal used in their production.

Supports/Goes against/No bearing

7 Henry believes the company is committed to its graduate recruitment programme.

*He hears one of his colleagues on the programme being praised by her manager.

Supports/Goes against/No bearing

8 Harriet thinks Henry is dissatisfied with his job.

*He does not arrive as early each morning as when he started last year.

Supports/Goes against/No bearing

9 Henry thinks one of the van drivers is stealing from the company.

*The van driver drives to work in an expensive new sports car.

Supports/Goes against/No bearing

10 Harriet believes that the company's Health and Safety policy is not being complied with.

*She sees a machinist receive a warning from the Production Manager for working without her safety goggles on.

Supports/Goes against/No bearing

11 Henry believes the company is committed to developing all of its staff.

*He finds out that about 55 per cent of the production staff have been on day-release courses.

Supports/Goes against/No bearing

12 Harriet believes that managers prefer not to eat with production staff in the restaurant.

*She notices that managers tend to eat together.

Supports/Goes against/No bearing

13 Henry thinks the travel, subsistence and accommodation expenses are unfair.

*He finds that they only just cover what he spends when he travels away from the office and stays overnight.

Supports/Goes against/No bearing

14 Harriet thinks that her manager is unfairly critical of her and her work.

*Her manager has recently rated her during her appraisal as competent at her job.

Supports/Goes against/No bearing

Instructions and practice questions for Section 3: Assumptions

This section assesses your ability to spot the assumptions people are making in what they are telling you. You are given remarks which are made to our trainee managers, Henry or Harriet. In each case the speaker may well be making assumptions, taking things for granted. You need to decide which of the statements you are presented with the speaker is definitely taking for granted.

You need to answer:

- **Must**: This means the speaker must necessarily/definitely be making this assumption.

- **?**: This means the speaker may or may not be assuming something is true.

Practice Questions:

Distribution manager to Harriet:

'Basic delivery routes are worked out by the software. It is quite sophisticated – it uses distances as well as average speeds for different times of day. But I think our experienced drivers are better off using their own judgment, for example about school holidays and half terms.'

P1 There is more traffic on the road when there is a school holiday.

Must/?

P2 The computer is able to calculate distances from the warehouse to a destination.

Must/?

P3 Drivers are better at devising a route than the software.

Must/?

The answers should be ?, Must, and Must respectively. P1 may well be true. We know there is a different level of traffic but not whether it is more or less. So there is nothing in the remark to suggest it is necessarily true. P2 and P3 must be based on the manager's assumptions.

Now turn the page and do the following questions. **You have eight minutes**.

Section 3: Questions

Accounts Manager to Henry:

'You need to get your last month's expenses in as quickly as possible, otherwise there is likely to be a delay this month.'

1 Henry has expenses to claim back this month.

Must/?

2 She is expecting a larger number of claims this month.

Must/?

Line Manager to Harriet:

'Could you leave home earlier tomorrow? The roadworks on the motorway are scheduled to start tomorrow.'

3 Harriet drives to work.

Must/?

4 The roadworks will cause delays.

Must/?

5 The motorway maintenance contractors are going to start on time.

Must/?

6 Harriet is a motivated employee.

Must/?

7 Harriet is likely to agree to this request.

Must/?

Production Manager to Henry:

'Teamworking arrangements have had a significant impact. When people are working together, are completely involved and more responsible for producing a product from start to finish, motivation goes up and so does productivity.'

8 It is a company's duty to ensure staff are well motivated.

Must/?

9 Henry agrees with the new working arrangements.

Must/?

10 Higher productivity leads to higher motivation.

Must/?

11 Teamworking arrangements have made the company more profitable.

Must/?

12 Teamworking arrangements lead to better industrial relations.

Must/?

13 Senior management agree with the new teamworking arrangements.

Must/?

Sales Manager to Harriet:

'We are losing market share to foreign imports. We need to improve quality as we will find it increasingly difficult to compete on price.'

14 Customers are more attracted by quality than price.

Must/?

15 Foreign imports are much cheaper than the company's products.

Must/?

16 Foreign imports are currently the same quality as the company's products.

Must/?

17 It is possible to improve the quality of the company's products.

Must/?

18 The company's market share will continue to decline.

Must/?

19 Foreign workers are paid less than those in the company.

Must/?

Production Manager to Henry:

'Our team leaders find the job very difficult, particularly if they were a team member of the team they are now leading. Even if they are leading a different team they often ask to go back to being ordinary team members, as they cannot cope with their new responsibilities.'

20 Team leaders find it easier to lead teams they were not members of.

Must/?

21 Team leaders often identify more with their colleagues in the team than with the management.

Must/?

22 Team leaders often cannot cope with their responsibilities.

Must/?

23 Team leaders lack adequate training to be a team leader.

Must/?

24 Team leaders often do not possess leadership qualities.

Must/?

25 Team leaders sometimes succeed in their new roles.

Must/?

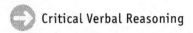

TEST 2: WATSON GLASER ITEM STYLE

This test is more difficult than the previous one. It simulates the demands of the tests developed by online test publisher Tests-Direct. Their tests are useful to include in this book as they assess a similar range of critical reasoning skills to those assessed by the most long-lived critical reasoning test – the Watson Glaser Critical Reasoning Appraisal. This test however involves reading a somewhat longer passage than you would be required to read by the Watson Glaser. The Watson Glaser involves displaying different critical reasoning skills on different pieces of information. This test involves displaying exactly the same types of evaluations as the Watson Glaser but on the same piece of information. This approach comes closest to how critical reasoning skills are actually demonstrated in the workplace.

This test is untimed but is likely to take you about 45 minutes. This means if you cannot spare the time to do it in one sitting you are able to stop and return to the test when you have more time.

Now begin. Read the passage on pages 49–50 and go on to do the questions.

Website

It seems that every major company now has a website. But judging by the variation in the quality of these websites, there does not seem to have been much understanding of the unique potential of a website and the interactivity that characterises this still relatively new form of communication with customers. Web technology has increased the speed at which many things can be done, particularly the accessing of information or the buying of products or services. Companies that fail to rise to this pace of change will lose the 'end users' or customers to the competition fast. If customers find information on web pages to be old, out of date or devoid of new information, they simply have no reason to return.

Organisations often underestimate the effect of a more interactive medium such as a website. Space needs to be given for response by email, which can be a very rich source of all-important consumer feedback and relatively cheap research. But in turn additional resources are required to deal with the extra workload a website generates. Information for the site should be customised, boiled down to as few pages as possible, coherently structured and well-presented. It should carry lots of interesting topics, elements of serendipity, plenty of places to go and search devices to speed up accessibility.

The web is a highly visual medium; there is a danger of design triumphing over content. How the information is arranged is the most important part of the design. Design is there to complement the content and help the user. It is imperative to engage, entertain and inform your website visitors.

Critical Verbal Reasoning

The web has not only improved business communication with its customers. By its very nature, it brings departments within companies with traditionally very different goals and workstyles closer together. Now information technology, finance, human resources departments, senior management, marketing, production, sales and distribution need to co-operate, collaborate and communicate closely to build a website that really works.

Section 1: Inferences

If you think the statement is already made in the passage or is implied or follows logically from the information given, mark your answer as **True**.

If you think the statement contradicts a statement made in the passage and so cannot be implied and does not logically follow from the information given, mark your answer as **False**.

If you think you do not have enough information to decide whether the statement is true or false based on the information given, mark your answer **Can't tell**.

Now turn over the page and begin.

1 Traditional communications media are more passive by comparison to web-based communications.

True/False/Can't tell

2 Websites have improved the delivery of customer services.

True/False/Can't tell

3 Website content should be 'end user' focused.

True/False/Can't tell

4 A website is closer to print than a broadcast medium.

True/False/Can't tell

5 The only set limitation on a website is the computer screen used to view it.

True/False/Can't tell

6 Consumers look for consistency in products and services but change on a website.

True/False/Can't tell

7 Websites can be used for customers to communicate directly with companies.

True/False/Can't tell

8 The website puts control of what is viewed and read into the hands of the viewer.

True/False/Can't tell

9 Websites are better at communicating information than any other media.

True/False/Can't tell

Section 2: Assumptions

If you *accept* what is stated below, based on the information given, mark your answer **Accept**.

If you *do not accept* what is stated below, based on the information given, mark your answer **Reject**.

Now turn over the page and begin.

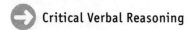

10 A company without a website risks rapidly losing business to competitors.

Accept/Reject

11 A well-designed website involves many icons and aesthetic graphics.

Accept/Reject

12 Once a site is launched most of the work involved is complete.

Accept/Reject

13 Companies act on information received via their websites.

Accept/Reject

14 The contents of a website can be regularly changed.

Accept/Reject

15 A website is not an ideal medium for lengthy detailed documents.

Accept/Reject

16 Information technology governs website content.

Accept/Reject

17 People are often interested in things they discover by chance.

Accept/Reject

18 A website can give an overview of a company.

Accept/Reject

Section 3: Deduction

If you decide that the statements below *necessarily follow* from the information given, mark your answer **True**.

If you decide that the statements below *cannot follow* from the information given, mark your answer **False**.

Now turn over the page and begin.

19 Websites have done more for internal communications than any training course could do.

True/False

20 As long as information is clearly signposted on the website, visitors will continue to return to your site.

True/False

21 The structure of information is what should govern the design of a website.

True/False

22 Search devices on websites indicate poor design.

True/False

23 Content should be created specifically for the web.

True/False

24 Companies are using websites to republish or repurpose information already available.

True/False

25 A website is an invaluable customer feedback tool.

True/False

26 A website is a key element in business communication.

True/False

27 Websites reduce the company's workload.

True/False

Section 4: Interpretation

If you think the statements below *are* justified and are likely to follow from information given, mark your answer **Agree**.

If you think the statements below *are not* justified and not likely to follow from the information given, mark your answer **Disagree**.

If you think you are *unable to agree or disagree* with the statements below based on the information given, mark your answer **Can't tell**.

Now turn over the page and begin.

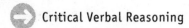

28 The time saved in transactions means few additional company resources are required to manage a website.

Agree/Disagree/Can't tell

29 The website is worth the investment as it is a very cost effective communications medium.

Agree/Disagree/Can't tell

30 Websites can undermine company security and confidentiality.

Agree/Disagree/Can't tell

31 The web is the biggest leap in customer communication for any company.

Agree/Disagree/Can't tell

32 More employees with specialist IT knowledge are required by companies with websites.

Agree/Disagree/Can't tell

33 Companies need to invest in additional training because of the demands created by a website.

Agree/Disagree/Can't tell

34 Everyone in business should have a website.

Agree/Disagree/Can't tell

35 A website can turn a national company into a global concern.

Agree/Disagree/Can't tell

36 Having a website improves business communication skills at all levels.

Agree/Disagree/Can't tell

Section 5: Evaluation of arguments

When we are having to make decisions we need to distinguish between arguments which are strong and those which are weak. This section involves making this distinction.

Based on the information given in the passage, if you think the arguments below *are important and directly related* to the passage, mark your answer **Strong**.

Based on the information given in the passage, if you think the arguments below *are neither important nor related* to the passage (although they may have more general relevance), mark your answer **Weak**.

Remember, try not to let your personal opinions or knowledge of the subject determine your answer.

Now turn over the page and begin.

37 Companies need to know what they want to communicate and who they want to reach with their website.

Strong/Weak

38 Consumers are in an age of information overload.

Strong/Weak

39 The full potential of many websites has yet to be realised.

Strong/Weak

40 Web technology has provided 24hr/7-days-a-week access to information.

Strong/Weak

41 It is important to have as many links as possible from your site to other related sites.

Strong/Weak

42 Website-dependent companies run a higher risk of fraud.

Strong/Weak

43 How a website is designed determines how well it functions as a communication tool.

Strong/Weak

44 A website can alienate the workforce.

Strong/Weak

45 Companies are still grappling with the interactive channels opened up by the web.

Strong/Weak

TEST 3: ASE/SHL/CIVIL SERVICE FAST STREAM ITEM STYLE

This test provides you with an opportunity to develop the skills required for the most widely-used critical verbal reasoning tests developed by two publishers, ASE and SHL. These include ASE's GMA (V), and SHL's VMG series. This item style is also identical to that found in the verbal element of the Civil Service Fast Stream Screening Tests developed by Cubiks.

This item style presents you with a passage followed by some related statements. You are then required to indicate whether, based on the information in the passage, the statement is true, false or can't tell. It helps to remember the point made in Chapter 1 – that the question statements are actually conclusions. They could all be prefaced by words such as thus, therefore, so, or hence. This means the task is essentially searching for reasons (statements made in the passage) which would enable you logically to draw the conclusions in the question statements. You are therefore required to demonstrate the ability to make three distinctions: True/False, True/Can't tell and False/Can't tell.

As with all critical reasoning tests the trick is to be able to make these distinctions in the face of quite persuasive, contentious or even emotive information, and to be able to put what you know or feel to one side and focus on what is in front of you in the passage. Many of the passages here have been deliberately chosen because they are about issues you may have quite strong personal beliefs about.

For the purposes of this test you need to operate on the following definitions:

- **True**: a statement has been made in the passage or logically follows from a statement or statements made in the passage.

- **False**: a statement contradicts a statement or statements which have either been made in or are implied by the passage, or a statement which would follow logically from the passage.

- **Can't tell**: this is where there is not enough information in the passage to make conclusions about the truth or falsity of the statements.

Try this example:

It has been estimated by the United States Federal Government that around ten million people in Latin America depend on the commercial production of the coca leaf, the plant which is refined to produce cocaine. Not all coca leaf cultivation leads to cocaine. For example, in Bolivia indigenous peoples chew coca leaf to boost energy levels in the same way many Europeans would drink coffee or tea.

The most profitable element of the cocaine 'supply chain' – turning the leaf into the powder – is controlled by a small number of 'cartels'. The income for growers provides a subsistence level of living. But more often than not the land used to cultivate the coca leaf is unsuitable for other crops. Cartels are highly organised and ruthless gangs who wield considerable political and economic influence in Latin America. The US

Federal Government believes the best way of reducing the use of cocaine in the US would be to encourage growers to move to other forms of subsistence farming.

Now answer these questions:

P1 Elected governments in Latin America are opposed to the activities of the cartels.

True/False/Can't tell

P2 The US Federal Government is opposed to cocaine production.

True/False/Can't tell

P3 Farmers grow coca leaf rather than other cash crops because of the higher income the crop provides.

True/False/Can't tell

P4 US Federal government policy is likely to be successful.

True/False/Can't tell

The answers to the example questions are:

P1 Can't tell. Although you might have been tempted to put False as we are told the cartels wield considerable political influence, we are not actually told anything about the policies of Governments in Latin America, so the answer is Can't tell.

P2 True. You may have been tempted by the Can't tell option here as there is no specific statement about US Federal Government policy. But the statement here is implied by the policy initiative aimed at encouraging growers to switch to other crops.

P3 False. We are told here that the land is generally unsuitable for any other form of cultivation.

P4 False. On the basis of the information provided in the passage it follows that the policy is unlikely to be successful. The farmers appear to have no other option.

Now turn the page. You have 30 minutes to do the following questions.

Perhaps the most important aspect of social gendering concerns technology and skills. One argument has emphasised the powerful affinity between men and machines; 'the identification of men with technology and of technology with masculinity'. This is partly a cultural process operating well beyond the confines of the workplace. Technology, it is argued, enters our social identity; femininity is incompatible with technical competence; so to feel technically competent is to feel manly. Thus technology is a 'medium of power' and by colonising technology men are claiming power for themselves and also power over women.

1 A woman with technical competence will feel manly.

True/False/Can't tell

2 All men have an interest in technology.

True/False/Can't tell

3 Our social identities have been changed because of the pursuit of power through technology.

True/False/Can't tell

4 Power is not accumulated through technical competence.

True/False/Can't tell

The social construction of sexual identity is embedded in organisational and work practices. A gendered organisational culture produces divisions of work rewards and power; a set of symbols and language that reinforces these differences; a set of daily practices and exchanges that dramatise and recreate the differences between the sexes; a set of beliefs and values that are being continually reinforced.

5 A gendered organisation will use language which reinforces gender divisions within it.

True/False/Can't tell

6 Organisational culture does not reinforce differences between genders.

True/False/Can't tell

7 Men are likely to have greater power and responsibility at work.

True/False/Can't tell

8 For those who have jobs, sexual identity is mainly dependent on the organisational culture of where they work.

True/False/Can't tell

A recent push by the UK government to boost women's struggle for equal pay or opportunities came with a report published in 2006. This independent review of women's employment and pay looked at the business case and more general importance for utilising 'human capital'. Women often outperform men in universities and schools; so it makes little sense if this asset and the investment in women's education is wasted by crowding women into low-paid jobs and seeing them under-represented at all levels of management. The 'business imperative' of employing the best people in pursuit of value creation demands that talent is employed to the full.

9 Women should have their salaries increased as they have greater educational and academic achievements.

True/False/Can't tell

10 The 'business imperative' means women should be employed in greater numbers over men.

True/False/Can't tell

11 More women are in low-paid jobs due to the high percentage of women that work part-time.

True/False/Can't tell

12 There are slightly more than 50 per cent of women at management level.

True/False/Can't tell

Research into the activities and policies of federal agencies of the United States Government who were operating in New York ostensibly to help the blind provides a telling illustration of how organisations in practice simply adapt to whatever environment they find themselves in. It was discovered that 80% of the registered blind are multi-handicapped, elderly and black and that these groups were relatively ignored by these welfare agencies. The agencies were mainly interested in the 'desirable blind', those who were young, white and employable – as this group was more appealing to fundraisers and easier to deal with.

13 Welfare agencies tend to discriminate racially.

True/False/Can't tell

14 The study found federal agencies for the blind in New York were only interested in a fifth of the registered blind.

True/False/Can't tell

15 The registered blind in New York are treated equally when they apply for welfare support from federal agencies.

True/False/Can't tell

16 The federal agencies adapted their strategies to suit the needs of the client group.

True/False/Can't tell

The year 2004 saw, temporarily at least, the return of the strike to UK industrial relations. Increasingly strikes have been pictured as outdated relics of a bygone industrial age, inappropriate to modern organisations and working patterns. Yet in 2004 1.3 million working days were spent on strike. This was the highest figure recorded for 14 years. This may have been a temporary upsurge, since in 2005 strikes fell again to 497,000 working days lost through strikes. But according to surveys, employers and labour leaders both predict renewed levels of strike activity.

17 In 2005 strike activity was slightly over a third of that of the previous year.

True/False/Can't tell

18 In 1991 strike action was reduced from the previous year.

True/False/Can't tell

19 Strikes will continue to rise after 2005.

True/False/Can't tell

20 The labour market and skill shortages strengthened the power of workers and led to the upsurge in strikes in 2004.

True/False/Can't tell

One noted study of what the author termed 'insidious power' was an examination of the practices and procedures in mental institutions. It showed how treatment could be used by hospital staff as a punishment rather than a cure and how doctors often withheld treatment until patients had accepted the psychiatric diagnosis of their condition. Furthermore, patients' apparently bizarre behaviour could often be interpreted as attempts to gain a few basic rights (such as a degree of privacy) denied them in the artificial conditions of the asylum. The psychiatric profession usually regarded this as further evidence of the patient's illness thus reinforcing and deepening the patient's powerlessness.

21 The hospital staff often reinforced their power over patients by their interpretation of patients' behaviour.

True/False/Can't tell

22 Treatment was never given until a patient had accepted their illness.

True/False/Can't tell

23 A patient's mental health was mostly dependent on the punishment he or she received from staff.

True/False/Can't tell

24 Access to basic rights such as privacy was dependent on the patient's behaviour.

True/False/Can't tell

For Freud, the unconscious was more than just a crucial psychological concept that explained a range of psychological phenomena. For him, it was culturally much more significant. For him, it represented 'the third blow to the narcissism of man'. Copernicus – who showed the earth was not the centre of the universe – had delivered the first. Darwin struck the second, when he demonstrated that we were descended from primates. The unconscious was the third blow because it undermined the comfortable notion of man being rational and self-aware. In a century in which Freud and millions of others had sons in the trenches and in which he had to flee the Gestapo, the truth of this seemed only too obvious.

25 War is good evidence for discarding the notion of man as rational.

True/False/Can't tell

26 Freud believed the concept of the unconscious dented our view of mankind as a rational being.

True/False/Can't tell

27 The unconscious was not used by Freud as an explanation of some psychological phenomena.

True/False/Can't tell

28 Man is innately narcissistic.

True/False/Can't tell

Feminist psychologists have for some time argued that multi-role conflicts are particularly acute for women attempting to juggle domestic and occupational commitments, and especially for women who are educationally accomplished and so expected to succeed occupationally. The way in which women deal with the stress associated with role conflicts is by performing what is referred to as 'psychological gymnastics'. These involve extremely complex trade-offs and juggling of domestic and occupational responsibilities. It has been suggested that women were rather too skilled at performing such gymnastics for their own good.

29 'Psychological gymnastics' are performed only by women.

True/False/Can't tell

30 Women who have greater academic achievements are likely to experience to a greater degree the stress caused by role conflicts than women with poor educational results.

True/False/Can't tell

31 Men are just as good at juggling domestic and occupational commitments.

True/False/Can't tell

32 Women are not effective at dealing with the impacts of multi-role conflicts.

True/False/Can't tell

Japanese ascendancy has been attributed to many factors, among them cultural and historical influences. Japan was a feudal society until little more than a hundred years ago and came quickly into the industrialised era. This was thought to provide tight, vertically-integrated industrial and financial structures. In particular, the broad cultural factors with which Japanese society seems imbued – the extreme diligence and self-sacrifice of workers (the supposed Japanese ethic of 'living to work') and the capacity to identify with common goals at all levels of the organisation – have been regarded as the bedrock of Japan's phenomenal success.

33 Japan's industrial ascension took a fraction of the time of the UK's, in part because of the tightly-integrated industrial and financial structures.

True/False/Can't tell

34 Japanese workers believe they work to live.

True/False/Can't tell

35 Japanese workers' self-sacrifice has in part allowed Japan to move swiftly into and through the industrial era.

True/False/Can't tell

36 All feudal societies could achieve rapid industrialisation – i.e. in less than a hundred years.

True/False/Can't tell

Foucault, the French philosopher, identified older, archaic forms of power as being 'sovereign power' which usually emanated from the monarch and is the power that forms a kind of superstructure on a society. Foucault developed this theme using a historical analysis of criminality. Up until the eighteenth century, punishment involved elements of torture and public spectacle, such as the stocks, execution and the chain gang. The point about such punishment, Foucault argues, is that they were symptoms of a particular kind of power. A policy of terror and atrocity against the wrongdoer represented the sovereign exacting vengeance and was designed to make people aware of that power.

37 The stocks were commonly used as a method of imposing power through fear in the 1800s.

True/False/Can't tell

38 Sovereigns used torture against wrongdoers as an expression of their power.

True/False/Can't tell

39 Other kinds of power, those which are not 'sovereign power', will not involve punishment.

True/False/Can't tell

40 The modern day jail sentence is a symptom of the degraded power of the sovereign.

True/False/Can't tell

Research has suggested that a complex developmental pathway determines an individual's leadership motivation. For example, one view is that childhood experiences might affect leadership motivation. These experiences would include the extent to which teachers recognise and nurture leaders. This suggestion resonates with Freud's idea of the 'golden seed' – having someone tell us we have a special talent. Freud believed this experience was crucial because during times of stress and uncertainty we are able to refer back to it for reassurance.

41 Teachers are more likely to give special attention to those who demonstrate leadership potential.

True/False/Can't tell

42 When we are uncertain in a situation, reassurance can be found in our past experience.

True/False/Can't tell

43 Leadership motivation is made up of more than our past experience.

True/False/Can't tell

44 Those who have had the 'golden seed' planted in them go on to become leaders.

True/False/Can't tell

Machiavelli's advice was to make the pursuit of power itself the sole business of the leader. Gaining and retaining power was the only objective. In this form of 'pure politics' nothing was ruled out; all devices and stratagems, no matter how ruthless or underhand, were considered. Part of this message is that power exists on a different plane from normality; the sphere of power contains so many who are not good.

45 For Machiavelli the pursuit of power for a leader is absolute.

True/False/Can't tell

46 In 'pure politics' only the most devious methods are used.

True/False/Can't tell

47 In the sphere of power there is a greater percentage of evil over good people.

True/False/Can't tell

48 Machiavelli's advice was that moral values should be adhered to in the sphere of power.

True/False/Can't tell

Gender segregation is closely tied to the wide differences between male and female earnings. Studies have shown that only about half of the variation in pay can be attributed to lesser skills and training of women; the remainder reflects discriminatory practices – the concentration of women in jobs that attract poor pay because they are defined as low grade.

49 Variation in male and female salaries is not caused by discrimination.

True/False/Can't tell

50 Most women are in poorly-paid jobs.

True/False/Can't tell

51 Around 50 per cent of all variations in pay are due to women having been given less training and skills.

True/False/Can't tell

52 The majority of women have fewer abilities than their male counterparts.

True/False/Can't tell

Once a particular job or occupation becomes established as either men's work or women's work, the myths and prejudices about the relative abilities of the sexes become powerful justifications for retaining the status quo. Thus the supposed inferiority of women on attributes such as physical strength and mechanical aptitude has long justified their exclusion from skilled manual work. Also women's supposed lack of decisiveness and willingness to take responsibility are often the justification for excluding them from managerial and supervisory positions.

53 Perception of abilities or aptitudes that relate to gender prevent an 'open', 'fairer' labour market.

True/False/Can't tell

54 Female managers often fail to take responsibility.

True/False/Can't tell

55 If jobs were not 'gendered' women would be able to perform skilled manual labour.

True/False/Can't tell

56 Myths and prejudices about the relative abilities of the sexes are not powerful justifications for maintaining the status quo.

True/False/Can't tell

Managers can influence the evolution of culture by being aware of the symbolic consequences of their actions and by attempting to foster desired values. These values are what lie at the heart of a corporate culture. Management gurus argue that these values should be strongly held and openly supported because identification with other things, such as a Trade Union, can mean a weak or fragmented organisational culture. But managers can never control culture in the sense that many management writers advocate. However, an understanding of organisations as cultures opens our eyes to many crucial insights that elude other metaphors, but they do not always provide the easy recipe for solving managerial problems that many managers and management writers hope for. Nonetheless the belief has become firmly established that culture fosters success.

57 If employees identify with a trade union this will cause a weak and fragmented culture in an organization.

True/False/Can't tell

58 Values are not the basis of an organisational culture.

True/False/Can't tell

59 Organisational cultures foster success.

True/False/Can't tell

60 Managers determine the culture of an organisation.

True/False/Can't tell

TEST 4: WATSON GLASER ITEM STYLE

In this final practice test we return to the item style found in the Watson Glaser. Again, an extended information passage is used. The reason for this is simply because the Watson Glaser Test uses all of the item styles you are likely to encounter whatever test you eventually have to do on the day.

As with Test 2, this test is un-timed and should take you about 40 minutes. As before, there is no requirement to do the test in one sitting. So if you are on a train and the journey ends, you can continue it some other time.

Now turn over the page, read the passage and answer the questions.

Heat

The speed of travel nowadays means the body has less time to adjust to the climatic changes in the country of destination. Extremes of temperature are hazardous to health and physical wellbeing. Illness from excessive heat can present itself without exceptionally hot weather. Strenuous physical activity or exercise can cause heat exhaustion in the unfit. Heat exhaustion is a killer. The normal body temperature is 37 degrees centigrade. Any physical activity generates heat. To maintain a normal body temperature heat must be lost. Sweating releases heat from the body by evaporation. In a climate where the temperature exceeds thirty degrees centigrade, ten to fifteen litres of sweat can be lost in a day without physical exertion. As water is lost, so is salt. If the body has not adjusted, this loss can result in heat cramps anywhere in the body and can be serious. Salt added to food can sufficiently replace the loss but should not be added to water. Dioralyte is a compound of minerals and salts lost through sweating and can be added to water as a safe alternative to salt. The body normally takes about 3 weeks to adjust to heat by reducing salt loss in perspiration by half. Blood vessels in the skin dilate and increase the amount of heat loss.

The amount of fluid intake – water, fruit juices or tea is important. Alcohol should be avoided because of its diuretic properties.

Being overweight makes the body less able to respond effectively to heat. Excessive sweating leads to abnormal fluid and salt loss, which can result in circulatory failure. The body experiences heat cramps and exhibits shock. Body temperature may be normal or slightly raised and, if untreated, the victim will lose consciousness.

Heat stroke, if untreated, can result in brain damage and death. The body's heat regulatory mechanism stops working and the body's temperature continues to rise leaving the brain to cook.

Section 1: Inferences

If you think the statements below *follow sensibly* from the information given mark your answer as **True**.

If you think the statements do not *sensibly follow* from the information given mark your answer as **False**.

If you think you *do not have enough information to decide* whether the statements below *do sensibly follow* or *do not sensibly follow* from the information given, mark your answer as **Can't tell**.

Now turn over the page and begin.

 Critical Verbal Reasoning

1 The slower you are in getting to your destination, the less adjustment your body has to make on arrival.

True/False/Can't tell

2 If your body temperature exceeds 37 degrees centigrade, Dioralyte will bring the temperature down to normal.

True/False/Can't tell

3 The use of anti-perspirants will bring the temperature down to normal.

True/False/Can't tell

4 Extremes of temperature, hot and cold, can have the same end result.

True/False/Can't tell

5 Physical activity is a major cause of a rise in the body's temperature.

True/False/Can't tell

6 Removal of clothing helps to maintain body temperature.

True/False/Can't tell

7 Heat exhaustion is caused by exceptionally hot weather.

True/False/Can't tell

8 The body loses salt before it loses water.

True/False/Can't tell

9 Any increase in the body's normal temperature leads to shock.

True/False/Can't tell

Section 2: Assumptions

If you *accept* what is stated below, based on the information given, mark your answer **Accept**.

If you *do not accept* what is stated below, based on the information given, mark your answer **Reject**.

Now turn over the page and begin.

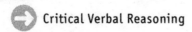

10 Overweight people have better chances of survival in cold climates.

Accept/Reject

11 Strenuous exercise is recommended before foreign travel.

Accept/Reject

12 Staying out of the sun prevents the body from overheating.

Accept/Reject

13 Alcohol intake increases fluid loss.

Accept/Reject

14 Heat exhaustion need not kill.

Accept/Reject

15 High body temperatures are present with heat stroke.

Accept/Reject

16 Water loss needs to be replaced on a regular basis.

Accept/Reject

17 No one can function without fluids.

Accept/Reject

18 Physical wellbeing is a factor in surviving heat stroke.

Accept/Reject

Section 3: Deductions

If you decide that the statements below *must follow* from the information given, mark your answer **True**.

If you decide that the statements below *cannot follow* from the information given, mark your answer **False**.

Now turn over the page and begin.

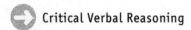

19 Sunburn leads to serious dehydration.

True/False

20 Excessive weight in hot climates causes excessive perspiration.

True/False

21 Your choice of holiday location should be informed by an assessment of your general health.

True/False

22 Healthy people sweat more than unhealthy people.

True/False

23 Physical activity generates heat loss.

True/False

24 Temperatures of 30 degrees centigrade and above require a 20 per cent increase in fluid intake.

True/False

25 Fruit juices are a vital source of vitamin and mineral intake and reduce the need for water.

True/False

26 Dioralyte is a safe water additive.

True/False

27 Heat cramps are the result of the body's inability to disperse excess heat.

True/False

Section 4: Interpretation

If you think the statements below *are* justified based on the information given, mark your answer **Agree**.

If you think the statements below *are not* justified based on the information given, mark your answer **Disagree**.

If you think you are *unable to agree or disagree* with the statements below based on the information given, mark your answer **Can't tell**.

Now turn over the page and begin.

28 Overweight people have larger sweat glands than underweight people.

Agree/Disagree/Can't tell

29 The larger the surface area of the skin, the greater the exposure to heat excess.

Agree/Disagree/Can't tell

30 Fitness rather than weight is a key factor in surviving hot climates.

Agree/Disagree/Can't tell

31 Fit people have a greater number of sweat glands than the unfit.

Agree/Disagree/Can't tell

32 Alcohol can replace fluids in the absence of other fluids in adverse climates.

Agree/Disagree/Can't tell

33 In extremes of heat all fluid loses should be minimised, including urination.

Agree/Disagree/Can't tell

34 The amount of heat loss increases when the blood vessels increase in size.

Agree/Disagree/Can't tell

35 The brain's ideal temperature to function is 37 degrees centigrade.

Agree/Disagree/Can't tell

36 The diuretic properties of alcohol aid water retention.

Agree/Disagree/Can't tell

Section 5: Evaluation of arguments

When we have to make decisions we need to distinguish between arguments which are strong and those which are weak. This section involves making this distinction. Based on the information given in the passage, if you think the arguments below *are important and directly related* to the passage, mark your answer **Strong**.

Based on the information given in the passage, if you think the arguments below *are neither important nor related* to the passage (although they may have more general relevance), mark your answer **Weak**.

Remember, try not to let your personal opinions or knowledge of the subject determine your answer.

Now turn over the page and begin.

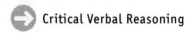

37 The speed at which we travel is a major contributor to heat exhaustion.

Strong/Weak

38 The internal body clock regulates body temperature.

Strong/Weak

39 Suntan lotion reduces the risk of sunburn.

Strong/Weak

40 Long haul travelling to hot countries is damaging the ozone layer and should be discouraged by governments.

Strong/Weak

41 Salt is a precious commodity in many cultures where there is a hot climate.

Strong/Weak

42 An untreated victim with heat cramps can go into shock.

Strong/Weak

43 Heat cramps are caused by the body's loss of salts.

Strong/Weak

44 In hot climates, brain damage is a result of the internal thermostat failing to control body temperature.

Strong/Weak

45 Pharmaceutical companies make excessive profits from Dioralyte.

Strong/Weak

CHAPTER 3

Answers to timed tests

TEST 1

Section 1: Analysis

1	Can't tell	**12**	Can't tell
2	True	**13**	False
3	True	**14**	True
4	False	**15**	Can't tell
5	True	**16**	True
6	Can't tell	**17**	False
7	True	**18**	Can't tell
8	False	**19**	Can't tell
9	False	**20**	True
10	False	**21**	True
11	True		

Section 2: Evaluation

1	Supports	**3**	No bearing
2	Goes against	**4**	Supports

5 No bearing

6 Supports

7 No bearing

8 No bearing

9 No bearing

10 Goes against

11 No bearing

12 No bearing

13 Goes against

14 Goes against

Section 3: Assumptions

1 Must

2 ?

3 Must

4 Must

5 Must

6 ?

7 ?

8 ?

9 ?

10 ?

11 ?

12 ?

13 ?

14 ?

15 Must

16 ?

17 Must

18 ?

19 ?

20 ?

21 ?

22 Must

23 ?

24 Must

25 Must

Critical Verbal Reasoning

TEST 2

Section 1: Inferences

1	True	**6**	Can't tell
2	Can't tell	**7**	True
3	True	**8**	Can't tell
4	Can't tell	**9**	Can't tell
5	Can't tell		

Section 2: Assumptions

10	Accept	**15**	Accept
11	Reject	**16**	Reject
12	Reject	**17**	Accept
13	Reject	**18**	Accept
14	Accept		

Section 3: Deduction

19	False	**24**	True
20	False	**25**	True
21	True	**26**	True
22	False	**27**	False
23	True		

Section 4: Interpretation

28 Disagree

29 Can't tell

30 Can't tell

31 Agree

32 Can't tell

33 Can't tell

34 Can't tell

35 Can't tell

36 Disagree

Section 5: Evaluation of arguments

37 Strong

38 Strong

39 Strong

40 Strong

41 Weak

42 Weak

43 Strong

44 Weak

45 Strong

TEST 3

1 True

2 Can't tell

3 Can't tell

4 False

5 True

6 False

7 Can't tell

8 Can't tell

9 Can't tell

10 True

11 Can't tell

12 False

13 Can't tell

14 True

15 False

16 False

17 True

18 True

19	Can't tell	**40**	Can't tell
20	Can't tell	**41**	Can't tell
21	True	**42**	True
22	False	**43**	False
23	Can't tell	**44**	Can't tell
24	Can't tell	**45**	True
25	True	**46**	Can't tell
26	True	**47**	Can't tell
27	False	**48**	False
28	Can't tell	**49**	False
29	Can't tell	**50**	Can't tell
30	True	**51**	True
31	Can't tell	**52**	Can't tell
32	False	**53**	True
33	Can't tell	**54**	Can't tell
34	False	**55**	Can't tell
35	True	**56**	False
36	Can't tell	**57**	Can't tell
37	False	**58**	False
38	True	**59**	Can't tell
39	Can't tell	**60**	False

TEST 4

Section 1: Inferences

1	True	**6**	Can't tell
2	False	**7**	False
3	Can't tell	**8**	False
4	True	**9**	Can't tell
5	False		

Section 2: Assumptions

10	Reject	**15**	Reject
11	Reject	**16**	Accept
12	Reject	**17**	Accept
13	Accept	**18**	Accept
14	Accept		

Section 3: Deductions

19	False	**24**	False
20	False	**25**	False
21	True	**26**	True
22	False	**27**	True
23	False		

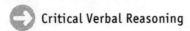

Section 4: Interpretation

28 Can't tell   **33** Can't tell

29 Can't tell   **34** Agree

30 Disagree   **35** Agree

31 Can't tell   **36** Disagree

32 Disagree

Section 5: Evaluation of arguments

37 Strong   **42** Strong

38 Strong   **43** Strong

39 Weak   **44** Strong

40 Weak   **45** Weak

41 Weak

CHAPTER 4

Explanations of timed tests

TEST 1

Section 1: Analysis

1 Can' tell. You may have put False – that non-employees cannot be members. But it is actually not clear from the information given whether non-employees can become members.

2 True. It is clear from the information that employees need a parking permit.

3 True. There are eleven days until the last Friday of the month.

4 False. You may have put True. Many of us have worked in settings where company policy and what actually happens are two very different things. But we need to put our beliefs (or cynicism) to one side in this instance and base our response on what is in front of us in the information given. This states that all non-compliance will be treated as a disciplinary matter and so the answer is False.

5 True. Although there is nothing specifically about smoking in the warehouse, suggesting Can't tell, we are told that the no-smoking policy is part of the Health and Safety Policy and that breaches result in disciplinary action.

6 Can't tell. It would be sensible if he was. But the document does not actually say, so the answer has to be Can't tell.

7 True. The subsidy implies that it could not run on a self-financing basis.

8 False. This might appear like a Can't tell. However, on the information provided, the entitlement does not go beyond 30 days. The answer has to be False.

9 False. If you got this one wrong, the most likely reason is that you simply did not read the statement carefully enough. It is the discount which applies at this rate.

10 False. The documentation indicates there are membership vacancies every year.

11 True. The company is clearly encouraging involvement in the committee.

12 Can't tell. Again, our knowledge of human nature may have led you to say True. But on the basis of the information given we have to say Can't tell.

13 False. He or she probably ought to. But the information tells us that the committee takes the decisions. So the answer has to be False. Even if he or she was a member of the Committee, the word 'major' implies this is not likely to be the case.

14 True. There is nothing stated or implied by the information that sports membership is a requirement.

15 Can't tell. This may well be true. But again we are not given any information which would make this a logical inference.

16 True. Only director level managers can park outside the office.

17 False. If you put True then you missed the fact that visitors' cars are also parked here. The answer is therefore False.

18 Can't tell. The answer here, despite whatever experience you have, is Can't tell. There is no definite reference to factory workers having an earlier lunch hour.

19 Can't tell. This is plausible given the policy which provides extra holidays. But strictly speaking we actually do not know from the information given here, so the answer has to be Can't tell.

20 True. There will be one Friday a month when weekly- and monthly-paid staff are paid together.

21 True. This appears to be true on the basis of the information given. Only air travel needs to be authorised; accommodation is reimbursed, implying employees make these arrangements themselves.

Section 2: Evaluation

1 Supports. It is reasonable to assume that, if the company is funding this trip, it will expect some return on the investment and some sales from the Latin American market.

2 Goes against. We have to assume if he was interested he would read the article.

3 No bearing. Retirement is determined by age rather than length of service.

4 Supports. There appears to be a relationship between the two facts. Although there may be other reasons for increased profits, the requirement here is that a fact merely supports the conclusion.

5 No bearing. The costs might appear to be a relevant fact to support this conclusion. But this conclusion – that the distribution centre will be closed – involves having to introduce too many other assumptions.

6 Supports. Although there will inevitably be other costs, the facts do at least support her belief.

7 No bearing. This fact does not provide any support for the conclusion. To say Supports would be to make the mistake of drawing a general conclusion (that the company supports its graduate recruitment programme) from a single fact (the conversation).

8 No bearing. This conclusion again goes well beyond what can reasonably be inferred from this fact. To interpret the arrival time as dissatisfaction with the job is to over-interpret this behaviour.

9 No bearing. Again this conclusion – theft from the company – goes well beyond what can be reasonably inferred from the ownership of the vehicle.

10 Goes against. It is unreasonable to infer non-compliance from this observation. If the Production Manager had ignored the health and safety issue, then this would have supported the belief.

11 No bearing. To say Supports would again be to commit one of the fallacies in reasoning – drawing a general conclusion – commitment to all staff development from one case (the training of production workers).

12 No bearing. This may seem initially like Supports – the managers eat together so surely this must support the belief they do not like to eat with the production staff. But it would be a case of over-interpreting this fact. Eating together with other manager does not support the idea that they do not like to eat with production staff.

13 Goes against. He is reimbursed what he spends.

14 Goes against. Being rated as competent does not support her belief.

Section 3: Assumptions

1 Must. She must be assuming he has expenses to reclaim.

2 ?. Although it appears that she must be assuming there will be a large number of claims this month, there may well be other reasons for a potential delay, such as reduced capacity in the accounts department caused by illness or staff holidays.

3 Must. The Line Manager must be assuming that she drives to work if the discussion is about roadworks on the motorway and journey time.

4 Must. The Line Manager must be assuming this, otherwise he or she would not be making the request.

5 Must. The Line Manager must be assuming they will start on time to make the request.

6 ?. He or she is making the request to leave home earlier, but this may or may not be based on the assumption that Harriet is motivated.

7 ?. The Line Manager is not necessarily assuming that Harriet will acquiesce. She may have domestic responsibilities which may make it difficult for her to leave home earlier.

8 ?. There are no grounds for thinking the Production Manager is necessarily assuming that it is the company's duty to ensure staff are motivated.

9 ?. The Production Manager is not necessarily assuming that Henry agrees with the new working arrangements.

10 ?. What the Production Manager is saying actually supports the reverse of this proposition – higher motivation leads to higher productivity.

11 ?. There is nothing to suggest there is an assumption about profit.

12 ?. There is nothing to suggest that the Production Manager is necessarily assuming better industrial relations follow.

13 ?. There is nothing in what the Production Manager is saying to suggest this is necessarily what is being assumed – there may well be considerable misgivings in some senior managers about the new arrangements.

14 ?. Quality and price appear to be important. The Sales Manager does not necessarily appear to be assuming one is more important than the other.

15 Must. The Sales Manager must be assuming the imported products are cheaper.

16 ?. This may look like a Must, but there is not sufficient information in the statement to mean the manager is definitely or necessarily assuming this. So the answer is ?.

17 Must. The Sales Manger must be assuming it is possible to improve quality.

18 ?. The Sales Manager is assuming the decline is remediable.

19 ?. The Sales Manager is not necessarily making this assumption. Goods could be cheaper because of subsidies, investment and productivity.

20 ?. It is not clear that the Production Manager is necessarily assuming team leaders would find it easier to lead teams they were not previously members of.

21 ?. The manager is not necessarily assuming that they identify more with their teams than the management.

22 Must. The manager must be assuming that they often cannot cope with their new responsibilities.

23 ?. The manager is not necessarily assuming they lack adequate training.

24 Must. The manager must be making this assumption about the leadership qualities of team leaders.

25 Must. The manager is assuming some do succeed.

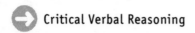

TEST 2

Section 1: Inferences

1 True. The inference follows from this being 'a more interactive medium.'

2 Can't tell. Although this might be the case there is nothing actually in the piece about the impact on customer services.

3 True. This is implied by reasons in the passage suggesting the website should help the user, as well as engage and entertain.

4 Can't tell. There is nothing in the passage which would support or negate this conclusion.

5 Can't tell. There are no reasons provided in the passage which would support this conclusion.

6 Can't tell. This may be the case. But there is no specific evidence about what consumers look for.

7 True. This is implied by the fact that customers can email organisations.

8 Can't tell. On the basis of the information given in the passage there is nothing which would enable us to conclude this.

9 Can't tell. This might seem like it is true, but we actually can't tell on the basis of the information given.

Section 2: Assumptions

10 Accept. On the basis of the information given here, Accept is justified. We are told that companies need to rise to the pace of change or lose their customers.

11 Reject. There is no reason given which would enable us to conclude that this is true.

12 Reject. This is quite clearly not the case based on the information given. Companies need to provide fresh, new information on a website.

13 Reject. Companies should respond, but we are actually being asked whether they do or not.

14 Accept. We are told that customers will not come back otherwise. So we can accept this reason as highly relevant to this conclusion.

15 Accept. We are told that website content should be boiled down to as few pages as possible. This represents a valid reason for accepting the conclusion.

16 Reject. We are clearly told that content is determined by the organisation.

17 Accept. We are told there should be an element of serendipity in a website, suggesting people are interested in what they discover by chance.

18 Accept. This is implied by the need for departments to work together.

Section 3: Deduction

19 False. We are told that websites could potentially get departments to work together, not that this has actually in reality happened.

20 False. We are told what is important is whether the information is changed regularly, is engaging and entertaining.

21 True. We are told that how the information is designed is what should govern the website.

22 False. We are told that good websites ought to include search devices.

23 True. We are told the information needs to be customised, making the question represent a valid conclusion.

24 True. We are told that information (which we assume already exists) needs to be coherently structured and well presented.

25 True. It is stated in the passage that a website can be an important source of customer feedback.

26 True. The passage suggests companies will lose customers if their website is uninteresting.

27 False. The passage indicates a website can increase a company's workload.

Section 4: Interpretation

28 Disagree. Given the reason stated in the passage, 'additional resources are required', we have to disagree with this conclusion.

29 Can't tell. Although the piece is very positive about websites (and we are specifically told it is a cheap source of research) there is nothing in the passage about overall costs or comparisons with other media. So the answer has to be Can't tell.

30 Can't tell. Again, this has to be Can't tell. There is nothing in the passage which would justify this conclusion.

31 Agree. This is a conclusion which would be justified given the information in the passage. This is based on the interactivity which is claimed for the media and the increase in the speed at which things can be done.

32 Can't tell. It is not clear from the passage that websites mean more employees with specialist knowledge are inevitable.

33 Can't tell. The passage states that more resources are required to deal with the extra workload. But it is not clear if this involves training. So the answer is Can't tell.

34 Can't tell. The passage would seem to suggest this. But it is not clear whether the benefits apply to all businesses.

35 Can't tell. There is nothing specifically in this passage which would justify this statement, although we may think this could well be the case.

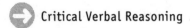

36 Disagree. The suggestion is that more co-operation and better communication will be required and not that this has already happened.

Section 5: Evaluation

37 Strong. This statement – knowing who and what has to be communicated – is directly relevant and important to the argument in the passage.

38 Strong. This is an important statement and relevant to the argument in the passage.

39 Strong. The statement – the full potential of many websites has yet to be realized – is directly relevant to the argument in the passage.

40 Strong. The statement – web technology has provided 24hr/7-days-a-week access to information – is relevant and important to the argument in the passage.

41 Weak. The number of links to related sites is not directly relevant or important to the argument in the passage.

42 Weak. The question of fraud is not directly relevant or important to the argument in the passage.

43 Strong. This statement is relevant to the issue of communicating effectively with customers using a website.

44 Weak. This statement is not directly relevant to the argument in the passage because the argument is not about alienation.

45 Strong. This statement is clearly relevant to the passage.

TEST 3

1 True. Although we may feel this ought not to be the case, the passage does actually state that to feel technically competent is to feel manly. So we have to conclude that a women with technical competence will feel manly, as no difference is stated between the impact of technical competence on men and women.

2 Can't tell. You may have answered True. The argument has emphasised the powerful affinity between men and machines – and identification of men with technology and of technology with masculinity. But the statement or conclusion is worded as an absolute: 'All men'. We cannot know on the basis of this passage that all men have an interest in technology.

3 Can't tell. We are told that technology enters our social identity (and may well change it). But the question is about the pursuit of power rather than technology.

4 False. The passage states that by colonising technology men are claiming power for themselves and that men are accumulating power through technology and technical competence. Therefore, in denying this, the statement is false.

5 True. This clearly follows from what we are told in the passage. The passage suggests that language, amongst other things, is used to reinforce gender differences.

6 False. We are told in the passage that differences between the genders are being continually reinforced. The question is therefore simply a restatement of this and so has to be true.

7 Can't tell. We may be tempted by the True option here – after all, this is seemingly what the passage implies and we may believe this to be the case from more general experience. But actually there is nothing in the passage which is explicitly related to the distribution of power and responsibility at work. So we have to conclude that we can't tell.

8 Can't tell. The passage tells us about the social construction of sexual identity in work and organisational practices. It does not have anything to say about how, more generally, our sexual identity is socially constructed.

9 Can't tell. This may seem like True. After all, we are told 'Women often outperform men in universities and schools; so it makes little sense if this asset and the investment in women's education is wasted by crowding women into low-paid jobs'. But while this statement suggests that women may perform better academically, it does not make the relationship between academic achievement and work performance and salary. Also the use of the word often means that not all women outperform men academically, but the conclusion is worded to suggest all women should have their salaries increased.

10 True. This is logically implied by the passage. We are told 'The business imperative of employing the best people in pursuit of value creation demands that talent is employed to the full'. In addition we are told 'Women often outperform men in universities and schools'. Therefore it is reasonable to assume more women should be employed than men.

11 Can't tell. Whilst we might be aware of other evidence which indicates that this is true, there is actually nothing in this passage indicating this is the case.

12 False. We are told in the passage that women are under-represented in management. So logically this suggests that there must be less than 50 per cent of managers who are women.

13 Can't tell. We may be tempted to say True. But the passage talks about welfare agencies in New York. There is nothing in the passage which actually tells us about the approach of welfare agencies more generally.

14 True. The passage suggests that '80% of the registered blind are multi-handicapped, elderly and black and that these groups were relatively ignored by the welfare agencies'. And we are told 'the agencies were mainly interested in the "desirable blind", those who were young, white and employable – as this group was more appealing to fundraisers and easier to deal with'. These reasons indicate that it follows that fundraisers would find 20 per cent of the blind more appealing.

15 False. For the same reasons as question 14, the conclusion can be considered false as those in the particular categories experience differences in treatment.

16 False. We are told 'the agencies were mainly interested in the "desirable blind", those who were young, white and employable – as this group was more appealing to fundraisers and easier to deal with'. This suggests the strategies were not based on the needs of the clients.

17 True. This may seem False, as the strikes have fallen between the two years. But the answer is True as the total number of days lost in 2005 is just over a third of what was lost in the previous year (2004).

18 True. This is implied by the statement that the 2004 figure is the highest ('This was the highest figure recorded for 14 years'). The passage indicates that 1990 was the previous highest level of strike activity, so in 1991 the strike activity must have been reduced, since the next highest level of strike activity was 2004.

19 Can't tell. This may seem like True as both employers and labour leaders are predicting an increase in strikes. But the question is not whether an increase is likely but whether more strikes will happen. We cannot tell for certain from the survey data that there will definitely be more strikes.

20 Can't tell. There is nothing in the passage which indicates what the possible reasons for this upsurge of militancy might be. So, despite what we may know from economics, we cannot conclude either true or false and so must go for Can't tell.

21 True. We are given a number of reasons which would support this conclusion: 'furthermore, patients' apparently bizarre behaviour could often be interpreted as attempts to gain a few basic rights [. . .] the psychiatric profession usually regarded this as further evidence of the patient's illness thus reinforcing and deepening the patient's powerlessness'.

22 False. The statement might seem true. But according to the information given here, doctors did not always withhold treatment. The passage merely states that 'doctors often withheld treatment until patients had accepted the psychiatric diagnosis of their condition'. So we have to conclude that the statement is false.

23 Can't tell. This might actually be the case but there is nothing in the passage which would conclusively suggests this.

24 Can't tell. Although the passage indicates that bizarre behaviour was an attempt to gain basic rights, there is nothing in the passage to definitively conclude either true or false here – i.e. that access was wholly dependent on their (the patients) behaviour; it is stated that bizarre behaviour is merely an attempt to gain access to basic rights.

25 True. We are told that 'in a century in which Freud and millions of others had sons in the trenches and in which he had to flee the Gestapo, the truth of this seemed only too obvious'. So whatever we may believe, the passage implies that this statement is true.

26 True. The passage states that for Freud it represented the third blow to the narcissism of man as it undermined the notion that we were rational and self-aware.

27 False. This contradicts statements made in the passage: 'the unconscious was more than just a crucial psychological concept that explained a range of psychological phenomena'. It was clearly used to explain some psychological phenomena.

28 Can't tell. We are told that 'it represented the third blow to the narcissism of man'. But the passage does not go as far as to indicate conclusively that man is innately narcissistic.

29 Can't tell. We are told about the way in which women deal with the anxieties associated with role conflicts. But we are told nothing about the way in which men

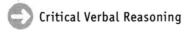

resolve these conflicts. So we are forced to conclude that
we cannot tell.

30 True. Whether this is true or not, we are actually told
that role stress is 'especially' experienced by women who
are educationally accomplished and so expected to
succeed occupationally.

31 Can't tell. We may believe this statement not to be
true – that men are worse at juggling occupational and
domestic commitments. We are also told that women are
'rather too good at psychological gymnastics for their own
good'. But there is nothing in the passage which would
enable us to conclude that men are either better or worse
than women at juggling occupational and domestic commitments.

32 False. We are told that 'women were rather too
skilled at performing such gymnastics for their own good'.
So we could conclude from this statement that the conclusion is false.

33 Can't tell. This may seem like true. We are told
'Japan was a feudal society until little more than a hundred
years ago and came quickly into the industrialised era',
and that 'This was thought to provide tight vertically-integrated industrial and financial structures'. But there is
nothing in the passage about industrialisation in the UK
which would enable us to conclude whether this was true
or false.

34 False. This question seeks to trick you into a True
response. The passage states that Japanese workers have
a very strong work ethic – they live to work rather than

work to live. So the conclusion directly contradicts a state-ment made in the passage and hence is false.

35 True. We are given a number of reasons. This state-ment follows from what we are told in the passage that 'extreme diligence and self-sacrifice of workers (the sup-posed Japanese ethic of "living to work") and the capacity to identify with common goals at all levels of the organisa-tion – have been regarded as the bedrock of Japan's phenomenal success'. This clearly enables us to conclude that, in part, Japan's success can be attributed to the self-sacrifice of its workers. It is also clearly implied that one of Japan's successes has been to move into the industrial era so quickly, therefore the link can be made.

36 Can't tell. This might seem like True, as after all Japan achieved it. But we are told there were other histori-cal and cultural factors which account for the rapid industrialisation. There is nothing in the passage about other feudal societies. So we are not able to conclude either true or false here.

37 False. We are told that 'up until the eighteenth century, punishment involved elements of torture and public spectacle, execution, the stocks and the chain gang. This implies that beyond the eighteenth century these punish-ments were not normal. Therefore a reasonable assumption is that they were not commonly used in the nineteenth century (1800–1899).

38 True. We are told that the policy of terror and atrocity against the wrongdoer was designed to make people aware of the sovereign's power. It can be assumed from this that they did use torture to express their power.

39 Can't tell. There is nothing in the paragraph that mentions other kinds of power, so we cannot assume they would not involve punishment.

40 Can't tell. Again there is nothing stated in the passage which mentions modern day sovereign power or if it has degraded, though one might assume from the media and observation that it has.

41 Can't tell. It is implied that teachers recognise and nurture leaders. The passage does not imply that only those who appear to have leadership potential are given special attention.

42 True. This is implied by statements made in the passage: 'This resonates with Freud's idea of the "golden seed" – having someone tell us we have a special talent', and 'Freud believed this experience was crucial because during times of stress and uncertainty we are able to refer back to it for reassurance'. We can assume the conclusion to be true as the conclusion here is that reassurance 'can' lie in our past experience and not that it always has to.

43 False. Whatever we may believe about where leadership motivation comes from, we are told that it is a developmental pathway which *determines* leadership motivation. The word 'determines' excludes all other possible causes.

44 Can't tell. Here we are making the distinction between necessary and sufficient conditions. The 'golden seed' may well be a necessary condition for leadership, (i.e. that all leaders have had the 'golden seed') but the passage does not imply that it is a sufficient condition (i.e. that this experience on its own will cause leadership motivation). So we have to conclude that we cannot tell.

45 True. This is implied by the statement 'Gaining and retaining power was the only objective'. From this reason we can view the conclusion as true, as gaining power was seen by Machiavelli as absolute and excluding all other objectives.

46 Can't tell. This might seem true. After all, we are told that 'in "pure politics" nothing was ruled out; all devices and stratagems, no matter how ruthless or underhand, were considered'. But the passage does not state conclusively that only these strategies should be employed. We cannot therefore arrive at a True or False response.

47 Can't tell. This again might seem true from a quick first reading of the passage. We are told that 'the sphere of power contains so many who are not good'. 'So many' here suggests an absolute number rather than a relative proportion. Therefore we cannot conclude either true or false here.

48 False. The statement that 'strategems, no matter how ruthless or underhand, were considered' clearly contradicts this conclusion.

49 False. This conclusion contradicts the statement that 'Studies have shown that only about half of the variation in pay can be attributed to lesser skills and training of women; the remainder reflects discriminatory practices'. It can be seen from the above reason that at least some of the variation in pay is linked to discrimination.

50 Can't tell. This may seem true as we are told that there is a 'concentration of women in jobs that attract poor

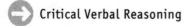

pay'. But whilst there is a higher proportion of women in lower paid jobs, it does not follow that, of all the economically active women across the labour market, the majority are in lower paid work.

51 True. Whilst we might not wish this to be the case, this conclusion follows straightforwardly from information in the passage: 'Studies have shown that only about half of the variation in pay can be attributed to lesser skills and training of women'.

52 Can't tell. We might wish to reject this obviously sexist statement. But there is actually nothing in the paragraph which tells us anything about the distribution of abilities in men and women. So we cannot conclusively reject or accept this statement.

53 True. This follows from statements made in the passage: 'Thus the supposed inferiority of women on attributes such as physical strength and mechanical aptitude has long justified their exclusion from skilled manual work'. We are also told that other attributes – decisiveness and lack of willingness to accept responsibility – affect access to managerial work. So the conclusion would have to be that perception of abilities and aptitudes prevents an open and fairer labour market.

54 Can't tell. We may think this definitely true or false. We may go for True because the passage may appear to support the view, i.e. women's supposed lack of decisiveness and willingness to take responsibility. Or we may think it is false simply on the basis of our personal experience. But the passage is about the impact of perception, myths and prejudices rather than reality. So ultimately we cannot tell.

55 Can't tell. Again, on the basis of our own beliefs, we may like to think this is either true or false. And the passage to some extent appears to support a false conclusion ('Thus the supposed inferiority of women on attributes such as physical strength . . .'). But there is not enough information here to conclusively accept or dismiss this conclusion, so we must go for Can't tell.

56 False. It may well be the case that the emotive appeal of this conclusion encouraged a True response. But this would directly contradict a statement in the passage. The passage states that myths and prejudices about the sexes are powerful justifications for maintaining the status quo.

57 Can't tell. You may have used the True response here. We are told that management gurus believe that identification with things other than the organisational values causes a weak and fragmented culture. However, beyond the gurus arguing this, there is no conclusive evidence here which would support what is actually a strong conclusion – that identification with unions *will* cause a weak and fragmented culture.

58 False. We are told that 'these values lie at the heart of a corporate culture'. So the conclusion here directly contradicts what follows from this statement.

59 Can't tell. There is a suggestion in the passage that cultures foster success. But this statement suggests that this is a belief which has become firmly established and not necessarily that this is actually the case. So we have to conclude Can't tell.

60 False. It may seem that this conclusion is true. We are told that managers can influence the evolution of a culture. But later in the passage we are also told that managers can never control a culture. In not being able to control the culture they are not, by implication, able to determine it.

TEST 4

Section 1: Inferences

1 True. The passage suggests that the speed of travel affects the time the body takes to adjust to climatic change, so the statement sensibly follows from this.

2 False. We are told Dioralyte replaces salts and minerals lost through sweating. It does not follow from this that it brings our temperature down.

3 Can't tell. Although we may think this is false we are not actually told anything about the impact of anti-perspirants on body temperature, so the answer is Can't tell.

4 True. Although the passage is largely about heat, we are told that 'extremes of temperature are hazardous to health and wellbeing'.

5 False. We are told that this is true in the unfit. The statement does not follow for all people.

6 Can't tell. There is actually nothing in the passage about the effect of removing clothing.

7 False. We are told that heat exhaustion can occur without exceptionally hot weather.

8 False. We are told that these happen simultaneously – 'as water is lost, so is salt'.

9 Can't tell. We are not told anything about whether there is a link between temperature and shock.

Section 2: Assumptions

10 Reject. We are told that being overweight makes the body less able to respond effectively to heat. We can reject this conclusion, as it does not follow from any statement in the passage.

11 Reject. This may seem like it is true. But this conclusion does not logically follow from any statement in the passage.

12 Reject. We are told that a number of factors cause the body to overheat. So we should reject this conclusion.

13 Accept. We are told that alcohol has diuretic properties, so the conclusion follows.

14 Accept. We are told that death is possible, but not inevitable ('if untreated'). So we can accept the conclusion.

15 Reject. The passage suggests the body temperatures associated with heat stroke can be normal.

16 Accept. The passage suggests water loss leads to heat cramps. So the conclusion follows from information in the passage.

17 Accept. We are told that fluid loss can result in circulatory failure and heat cramps. So it is reasonable to accept this conclusion.

18 Accept. We are told that being overweight makes the body less able to respond effectively to heat. We are also told that exercise can cause heat exhaustion in the unfit. Weight and fitness are components of physical wellbeing. So we can accept this conclusion.

Section 3: Deductions

19 False. This conclusion has no logical relationship with any of the statements in the passage.

20 False. We may believe this to be the case. But the information in the passage does not conclusively support the conclusion. We are told that excessive sweating leads to abnormal fluid and salt loss. But we are not told that this is caused by being overweight. Being overweight makes the body less able to respond effectively to heat. But we are not told what this ineffective response consists of.

21 True. This must follow from the information in the passage, as we are told that extremes of temperature are hazardous to health.

22 False. This does not follow from any information given in the passage.

23 False. We are told that any physical activity generates heat. So the conclusion must be false.

24 False. There is no information in the passage which would enable us to conclude that temperatures of 30 degrees centigrade or more require a 20 per cent increase in fluid intake.

25 False. We are simply told that fruit juices along with other fluids are important, not that they are a source of vitamins and minerals.

26 True. The passage states that Dioralyte is a safe alternative to salt. So the conclusion must be true.

27 True. This conclusion must follow from the combined effect of the statements in the passage. ('To maintain a normal body temperature heat must be lost. Sweating releases heat in the body by evaporation. . . . If the body has not adjusted [to climatic changes], this loss [of fluid] can result in heat cramps . . .').

Section 4: Interpretations

28 Can't tell. There is nothing in the passage about the size of sweat glands, So this must be Can't tell.

29 Can't tell. This may well be the case. But there is actually nothing in the passage about the impact of the surface area of the skin.

30 Disagree. This statement is not justified from information in the passage. We are told that both have an impact.

31 Can't tell. There is nothing in the passage which indicates what the number of sweat glands is in fit and unfit individuals.

32 Disagree. We are told that alcohol should be avoided because of its diuretic properties.

33 Can't tell. Whilst we are told that fluid intake is important and that fluid loss is dangerous, we are not actually told anything about the effect of urination, so the answer has to be Can't tell.

34 Agree. This conclusion is justified. We are told that the blood vessels dilate and increase the amount of heat loss.

35 Agree. This follows straightforwardly from the statement in the passage: 'the normal body temperature is 37 degrees centigrade'.

36 Disagree. This conclusion clearly contradicts the statement made in the passage about the diuretic properties of alcohol.

Section 5: Evaluations

37 Strong. We are told that the speed of travel means the body has less time to adjust to climate changes. So the conclusion is directly relevant to the argument in the passage.

38 Strong. This is relevant to the passage as it presents another factor which impacts on the effect of heat and travel.

39 Weak. This may well be true but it has little relevance to the information in the passage.

40 Weak. This may well be true but it is not directly relevant to the information in the passage.

41 Weak. This conclusion, although it may well be true, is not directly relevant to the passage.

42 Strong. This conclusion is directly relevant to information in the passage.

43 Strong. Again, this statement is straightforwardly relevant and related to information in the passage.

44 Strong. This statement is directly related to information in the passage.

45 Weak. The information in the passage is about the impact of speed of travel, adapting to climate change and the way the body copes with heat and fluid loss. The price charged for the supplement has little importance here.

CHAPTER 5

Diagnosis and further reading

INTERPRETING YOUR SCORE

How did you get on? In psychometric tests, the raw scores you achieve (the total number of correct answers for each of the tests) have little meaning. Performance is interpreted by comparing your score to the distribution of scores achieved by a comparison group.

As critical reasoning tests are 'high level' tests intended to differentiate the ability levels of those applying for supervisory and managerial roles, the comparison groups consist of managers. For Test 1, the comparison group is somewhat less senior. The group you are comparing yourself against here are people applying for team leader roles in a public sector organisation.

This use of fairly 'elite' comparison groups is an important point to bear in mind when considering your score. You are not being compared with the general population. So do not be too tough on yourself if you did not score as highly as you thought you would. These are demanding exercises rated against the score of managerial comparison groups.

The primary purpose of this book is to increase your confidence, critical reasoning skills and ultimately give yourself the best possible opportunity to do well on the day. It is not intended to give you precise feedback on ability levels.

Your score sits somewhere under the 'normal distribution curve' which, for simplicity, we split into five zones.

Test 1

Below Typical	0–28
Low Typical	29–33
Typical	34–38
High Typical	39–45
Above Typical	46+

Tests 2 and 4

To interpret your score for these tests combine your raw scores.

Below Typical	0–40
Low Typical	41–50
Typical	51–55
High Typical	56–65
Above Typical	66+

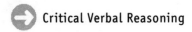

Test 3

Below Typical	0–23
Low Typical	24–29
Typical	30–35
High Typical	36–40
Above Typical	41+

SUGGESTIONS FOR FURTHER IMPROVEMENT

More practice

If you have enough time between now and the test session, have another go at the tests. In general, people's memory for test questions decays after about a month. So if you can leave a month between attempts you should have forgotten the correct and incorrect responses to questions.

Understanding and motivation

Study the detailed explanations of correct and incorrect responses. Try to understand why you got questions wrong. For example, did you find it difficult to put feelings, belief and knowledge to one side? The questions, particularly in Test 3, were often about subjects you may have strong feelings about.

Did you sometimes overlook the nuances in the way questions were worded? Critical reasoning tests define true and false in very particular ways. For example ASE's first graduate series defines it as being necessarily true (which means it has been stated in the passage). But the GMA (V) by the same publisher, simulated by Test 3, involves logical implication. So true here also means probably as well as necessarily.

It may also be useful to revisit the general advice at the end of Chapter 1. This provided some techniques for evaluating arguments such as putting conclusion words (so, thus, hence) in front of the questions, and reason words in front of statements in the passage (if, as).

Very often in management development programmes where critical reasoning has been identified as a development issue, people are told to go off and read more journals like *The Economist* or the serious newspapers where complex and persuasive arguments are presented. Of course studying and evaluating arguments in articles can help. But there are also books available which provide more focussed guidance and practice to improve technique. The best of these is Anne Thomson's *Critical Reasoning: A Practical Introduction* listed in the Further Sources of Practice section.

Remember, critical reasoning is an important life skill which is not just required to get through assessment processes. It is required in any job which involves evaluating evidence and decision-making. So the benefits of working through this set of practice exercises and becoming more aware of how you evaluate information should extend well beyond your test session.

ON THE DAY

You must plan to arrive at the test centre in a state that is conducive to achieving your best possible score. This means being calm and focused. It is possible that you may feel nervous before the test, but you can help yourself by preparing in advance the practical details that will enable you to do well. Remember, it is unlikely that you are the only person who is feeling nervous; what is important is how you deal with your nerves! The following suggestions may help you to overcome unnecessary test-related anxiety.

1 Know where the test centre is located, and estimate how long it will take you to get there – plan your 'setting off time'. Now plan to leave 45 minutes before your setting off time to allow for travel delays. This way, you can be more or less certain that you will arrive at the test centre in good time. If, for any reason, you think you will miss the start of the session, call the administrator to ask for instructions.

2 Try to get a good night's sleep before the test. This is obvious advice and, realistically, it is not always possible, particularly if you are prone to nerves the night before a test. However, you can take some positive steps to help. Consider taking a hot bath before you go to bed, drinking herbal rather than caffeinated tea, and doing some exercise. Think back to what worked last time you took an exam and try to replicate the scenario.

3 The night before the test, organise everything that you need to take with you. This includes test instructions, directions, your identification, pens, erasers, possibly your calculator (with new batteries in it), reading glasses, and contact lenses.

4 Decide what you are going to wear and have your clothes ready the night before. Be prepared for the test centre to be unusually hot or cold, and dress in layers so that you can regulate the climate yourself. If your test will be preceded or followed by an interview, make sure you dress accordingly for the interview which is likely to be a more formal event than the test itself.

5 Eat breakfast! Even if you usually skip breakfast, you should consider that insufficient sugar levels affect your concentration and that a healthy breakfast might help you to concentrate, especially towards the end of the test when you are likely to be tired.

6 If you know that you have specific or exceptional requirements which will require preparation on the day, be sure to inform the test administrators in advance so that they can assist you as necessary. Similarly, if you are feeling unusually unwell on the day of the test, make sure that the test administrator is aware of it.

7 If, when you read the test instructions, there is something you don't understand, ask for clarification from the administrator. The time given to you to read the instructions may or may not be limited but, within the allowed time, you can usually ask questions. Don't assume that you have understood the instructions if, at first glance, they appear to be similar to the instructions for the practice tests.

8 Don't read through all the questions before you start. This simply wastes time. Start with Question 1 and work swiftly and methodically through each question in order. Unless you are taking a computerised test where the level of difficulty of the next question depends on you correctly answering the previous question, don't waste time on questions that you know require a lot of time. You can return to these questions at the end if you have time left over.

9 After you have taken the test, find out the mechanism for feedback, and approximately the number of days you will have to wait to find out your results. Ask whether there is scope for objective feedback on your performance for your future reference.

10 Celebrate that you have finished.

FURTHER SOURCES OF PRACTICE

In this final part you will find a list of useful sources for all types of psychometric tests.

Books

Barrett, J., *Test Yourself! Test Your Aptitude, Personality and Motivation, and Plan Your Career*. London: Kogan Page, 2000.

Bolles, Richard N., *The 1997 What Colour Is Your Parachute?* Berkeley, CA: Ten Speed Press, 1997.

Carter, P. and K. Russell, *Psychometric Testing: 1000 Ways to Assess Your Personality, Creativity, Intelligence and Lateral Thinking*. Chichester: John Wiley, 2001.

Chin-Lee, Cynthia, *It's Who You Know*. Toronto, ON: Pfeiffer, 1993.

Cohen, D., *How to Succeed at Psychometric Tests*. London: Sheldon Press, 1999.

Crozier, G., *Test Your Verbal Reasoning*. London: Hodder & Stoughton, 2000.

Jackson, Tom, *The Perfect Résumé*. New York: Doubleday, 1990.

Jones, S., *Psychological Testing for Managers*. London: Judy Piatkus, 1993.

Kourdi, Jeremy, *Succeed at Psychometric Testing: Practice Tests for Verbal Reasoning (Advanced Level)*. London: Hodder & Stoughton, 2004.

Krannich, Ronald L. and Caryl Rae Krannich, *Network Your Way to Job and Career Success*. Manassa, VA: Impact Publications, 1989.

Nuga, Simbo, *Succeed at Psychometric Testing: Practice Tests for Verbal Reasoning (Intermediate Level)*. London: Hodder & Stoughton, 2004.

Parkinson, M., *How to Master Psychometric Tests*. London: Kogan Page, 1997.

Pelshenke, P., *How to Win at Aptitude Tests*. Kettering: Thorsons, 1993.

Rhodes, Peter S., *Succeed at Psychometric Testing: Practice Tests for Diagrammatic and Abstract Reasoning*. London: Hodder & Stoughton, 2004.

Smith, Heidi, *How to Pass Numerical Reasoning Tests: A Step-by-Step Guide to Learning the Basic Skills*. London: Kogan Page, 2002.

Thompson, A., *Critical Reasoning: A Practical Introduction*, 2nd edn. London: Routledge, 2002.

Tolley, H. and K. Thomas, *How to Pass Verbal Reasoning Tests*. London: Kogan Page, 2001.

Vanson, Sally, *Succeed at Psychometric Testing: Practice Tests for Data Interpretation*. London: Hodder & Stoughton, 2004.

Walmsley, Bernice, *Succeed at Psychometric Testing: Practice Tests for Numerical Reasoning (Intermediate Level)*. London: Hodder & Stoughton, 2004.

Walmsley, Bernice, *Succeed at Psychometric Testing: Practice Tests for Numerical Reasoning (Advanced Level)*. London: Hodder & Stoughton, 2004.

Walmsley, Bernice, *Succeed at Psychometric Testing: Practice Tests for The National Police Selection Process*. London: Hodder & Stoughton, 2005.

Williams, R., *Prepare for Tests at Interview for Graduates and Managers*. Cheltenham: NFER-Nelson, 1999.

Test publishers and suppliers

Assessment for Selection and Employment
Chiswick Centre
414 Chiswick High Road
London W4 5TF
telephone: 0208 996 3337

Oxford Psychologists Press
Elsfield Hall
15–17 Elsfield Way
Oxford OX2 8EP
telephone: 01865 404500

The Pscyhological Corporation
1 Proctor Street
London WC1V 6EU
telephone: 0207 911 1963

Saville & Holdsworth Ltd
The Pavilion
1 Atwell Place
Thames Ditton
Surrey KT7 0SR
telephone: 0208 398 4170

The Test Agency Ltd
Burgner House
4630 Kingsgate
Oxford Business Park South
Oxford OX4 2SU
telephone: 01865 402900

Useful websites

Websites are prone to change, but the following are correct at the time of going to press.

www.army.mod.uk/careers

www.armyjobs.co.uk

www.ase-solutions.co.uk

www.barcap.com/graduatecareers/barcap_test.pdf

www.bhgplc.com

www.bps

www.careerpsychologycentre.com

www.careers-uk.com

www.cipd.org.uk

www.deloitte.co.uk/index.asp

www.englishforum

www.englishtogo

www.ets.org

www.faststream.gov.uk

www.freesat1prep.com

www.guardian.co.uk/money

www.home.g2a.net

www.kogan-page.co.uk

www.mensa.org.uk

www.mod.uk/careers

www.morrisby.co.uk

www.newmonday.co.uk

www.oneclickhr.com

www.opp.co.uk

www.pgcareers.com/apply/how/recruitment.asp

www.police.uk

www.policecouldyou.co.uk

www.psychtests.com

www.psychtesting.org.uk

www.pwcglobal.com/uk/eng/carinexp/undergrad/quiz.html

www.publicjobs.gov.ie/numericatest.asp

www.puzz.com

www.rafcareers.com

www.rinkworks.com/brainfood.maths.html

www.royal-navy.mod.uk

www.testagency.co.uk

www.tests-direct.com

www.thewizardofodds.xom/math/group1.html

Weblinks

www.psychtests.com – free personality and ability/aptitude test to try out

www.psychtesting.org.uk – the British Psychological Society's resource site contains some helpful information for test takers

www.tests-direct.com – a useful commercial online provider's site offering inexpensive tests for a number of test types

Useful organisations

American Psychological Association Testing and Assessment

Association of Recognised English Language Schools (ARELS)

Australian Psychological Society

The Best Practice Club

The British Psychological Society

Canadian Psychological Society

The Chartered Institute of Marketing

The Chartered Management Institute

The Institute of Personnel and Development

Psyconsult

Singapore Psychological Society

Society for Industrial and Organisational Assessment (South Africa) (SIOPSA)

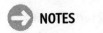 **NOTES**

NOTES

NOTES

SUCCEED AT

PSYCHOMETRIC TESTING

PRACTICE TESTS FOR DATA INTERPRETATION

SALLY VANSON

Are you about to attend an interview or assessment centre for a new job? Are you being considered for internal promotion or training? If so you may have to sit a psychometric or ability test. This book will help you to build the confidence and gain the skills needed to perform to the best of your ability under test conditions. **Data Interpretation** contains:

- Tips and advice on pre-test preparation
- Hundreds of new and original questions, and samples from SHL, a leading test provider
- Practice material for tests from all of the major test publishers which includes: data interpretation; graph interpretation
- Answers and clear explanations for each question
- A self-assessment section to analyse your scores and to measure your progress.

This book covers all levels of application from school leaver to post-graduate.

Sally Vanson is the Director of The Performance Solution, a consultancy specialising in training and development.

GET THE JOB YOU WANT TODAY

SUCCEED AT

PSYCHOMETRIC TESTING

PRACTICE TESTS FOR
NUMERICAL REASONING ADVANCED LEVEL

BERNICE WALMSLEY

Are you about to attend an interview or assessment centre for a new job? Are you being considered for internal promotion or training? If so you may have to sit a psychometric or ability test. This book will help you to build the confidence and gain the skills needed to perform to the best of your ability under test conditions. **Numerical Reasoning Advanced Level** contains:

- Tips and advice on pre-test preparation
- Hundreds of new and original questions, and samples from SHL, a leading test provider
- Practice material for tests from all of the major test publishers which includes: data interpretation; word problems; quantitative relations
- Answers and clear explanations for each question
- A self-assessment section to analyse your scores and to measure your progress.

This book will help you if you are a graduate or post-graduate currently working within higher management, or if you aim to work in this area.

Bernice Walmsley has had extensive experience of psychometric testing from her participation in a management development pro-gramme and in selection procedures for a major PLC.

GET THE JOB YOU WANT TODAY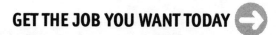

SUCCEED AT

PSYCHOMETRIC TESTING

PRACTICE TESTS FOR
DIAGRAMMATIC AND ABSTRACT REASONING

PETER S. RHODES

Are you about to attend an interview or assessment centre for a new job? Are you being considered for internal promotion or training? If so you may have to sit a psychometric or ability test. This book will help you to build the confidence and gain the skills needed to perform to the best of your ability under test conditions. **Diagrammatic and Abstract Reasoning** contains:

- Tips and advice on pre-test preparation
- Hundreds of new and original questions
- Practice material for tests from all of the major test publishers
- Answers and clear explanations for each question
- A self-assessment section to analyse your scores and to measure your progress.

This book covers all levels of application from school lever to post-graduate.

Peter S. Rhodes is a Chartered Psychologist and Director of Psychology at assessment consultancy OTL. He has authored a number of books on Work and Psychology.

GET THE JOB YOU WANT TODAY